Surrendered Hearts is a captivating book that will encourage, inspire, and enlarge your faith and trust in God, no matter what life experience you are facing! Lori Schumaker's authentic and heartfelt sharing, combined with her practical suggestions and biblical truth, is a must-read book for anyone who is adopting or struggling with surrendering their expectations of how life should be. Thank you, Lori, for touching my adoptive-mom heart, my grieving-a-child heart, and my longs-to-live-life-trusting-God heart, surrendered.

—Kathe Wunnenberg
President/Founder of Hopelifters Unlimited
Author of several books, including
Grieving the Child I Never Knew

This book is riveting! I couldn't put it down. Lori skillfully draws the curtain on international adoption and gives us a peek into the joys, sorrows, and unknowns that every adoptive family faces. She captivated me with her family's story while candidly sharing the faith lessons God taught her along the way. A must-read for everyone!

—Stefani Stoltzfus
Creator of the Truthbytes for Moms Bible study app
Author of *Mom on a Mission*
Blogger at *Walls of Home*
Adoptive mother and adoption advocate

Adoption is a surrendering. Giving to God what we cannot control. Trusting that God is working even when we cannot see, weaving together a family— many times against all odds. Lori Schumaker's new book, *Surrendered Hearts*, is a hope-filled story of adoption, and so much more. Lori's words remind us of the transformation found when we surrender our hearts to the loving Christ, trusting Him to move within the broken parts of our stories and letting Him make us new.

—Michelle Madrid-Branch, author, speaker
International adoptee
Global advocate for women and children
Host of the *Greater Than Podcast*

Wow! I loved this book! What an amazing journey that brought back many memories. I was inspired by Lori's unwavering faith and commitment to her daughter throughout her journey. With the many ups and downs in international adoption, the Schumaker's story shows how faith can overcome anything!

—SooJin Park
Program director and adoption case manager

As a pastor and a friend, I have had the privilege of walking with the Schumakers through this roller coaster of a journey. Watching their story unfold through the pages of this book gives me an even greater appreciation of this family's faithfulness and God's goodness. I have been challenged not simply to endure the journey but to embrace the joy that comes with learning to trust Jesus. Their story will inspire others to step confidently into a calling, whether it be adopting a child or changing a career path.

—Corey Bullock
Teaching and Next Generation pastor for
Trace Church of Colorado Springs
Former Gilbert and Ahwatukee Campus pastor for
Central Christian Church in Arizona

To my family—Bryan, Zachary, Landon, and Selah. This journey is about all of us. Together, we've faced fears, learned to surrender control, and trusted God. Through it, we've become stronger and our love deeper. To Selah, your story is a miracle, and we love you to the moon and back. To Zachary and Landon, your love for your sister blows me away. You are Selah's knights in shining armor and the protectors of her heart. And Bryan, you are exactly the kind of daddy every little girl needs—especially our Selah.

An Adoption Story
of Love, Loss, and
Learning to Trust

Surrendered
HEARTS

An Adoption Story of Love, Loss, and Learning to Trust

Surrendered HEARTS

LORI SCHUMAKER

© Lori Schumaker, 2018

Published by Redemption Press, PO Box 427, Enumclaw, WA 98022

Toll Free (844) 2REDEEM (273-3336)

Redemption Press is honored to present this title in partnership with the author. The views expressed or implied in this work are those of the author. Redemption Press provides our imprint seal representing design excellence, creative content, and high quality production.

Scripture versions used: NLT (10); NIV (8); ESV (5); BSB (3); MSG (1); AMP (1); GW (1)

ISBN: 978-1-68314-789-3
        978-1-68314-790-9 (ePub)
        978-1-68314-791-6 (Mobi)

Library of Congress Catalog Card Number: 2018959170

ACKNOWLEDGMENTS

I f you could look into the past and see who I was twenty-five years ago, you'd have difficulty recognizing me. Back then if you peeked below the surface of my smile, you'd find a broken girl. You'd see a believer, but not someone surrendering her life to Christ. You'd see hope, but not the kind of hope someone has when they trust Jesus with everything.

Today I'm different because I surrendered. Even though it's an ongoing journey, the difference is visible both emotionally and physically. As I've followed Him, God has broken chains and carried our family through things that would be impossible without Him.

Without our surrender—without trust enough to follow Him through the difficult times, we wouldn't be the family we are today. We wouldn't have walked the road of adoption. We'd have missed out on so many good things.

So today, I thank Jesus for everything. I thank Him for loving me when I was blinded, broken, and lost. And I thank Him for bringing people alongside me to minister to my heart and encourage me along the way. They make sharing Selah's story through this book possible.

Thank you, Bryan, for choosing me. For being the logic to my emotion and the laughter to my oh-too-serious self. Thank you for supporting my ministry and pushing me out of my comfort zone.

Thank you to my boys, Zachary and Landon. The way you love and encourage is way beyond your years. The perfectly timed hugs, texts, and cups of coffee each morning were just what I needed. Without them, this book would not be complete!

Selah, my sweet girl. My reminder to reflect on the goodness of God all the time. Thank you for being so brave. We are learning about this surrender thing together, aren't we? Thank you for teaching me to love better and trust more. I am so honored to be your mommy.

Thank you to my parents, who have always believed I'd write a book someday. Dad, you taught me about writing long ago and gave me that antique army typewriter. It birthed a dream in my heart.

To the Nolans. Thank you for your witness of faith. Col, you've walked me toward freedom and

ACKNOWLEDGMENTS

prayed for those chains to break. Thank you for that. And, Kourt, you are a priceless treasure and bring great joy to the world around you. Thank you for melting Uncle Bry's heart and teaching him what adoption is all about.

Thank you, All God's Children and SooJin Park. Our family is complete because of you. Thank you for all you do for children in need.

To my prayer warrior friends. Goodness, I'd never be here without you. You've prayed us up and over every mountain. LeAnne, you were my first real breath of Jesus with skin on when I was just a girl. My mom's group sisters, you did not relent but stormed heaven's gates for us!

Thank you, Central Christian friends, for not only praying us through the difficult times but for encouraging me to follow Jesus as He called. How faithfully you have stood by me!

To my Blessing Counters Sisters! Your prayers, encouragement, and wisdom keep me on track and remind me to trust in the great I Am.

Thank you, Athena and Redemption Press, for making this book possible. Athena, our God moment in the airport inspired me to take out the story I had long put away. You are a gift.

SURRENDERED HEARTS

And finally, thank you, Yvonne and Monica. Your willingness to step beyond yourselves changed our lives. You allowed God to use you as His conduit, and because of that we are a family today. I am forever grateful.

Table of Contents

Introduction. 15

The Surrendered Heart Manifesto 17

Part 1: God Prepares Us

Chapter 1: Why Adoption? 21

Chapter 2: The Story Began Long before We Knew . .25

Part 2: Our Miracle

Chapter 3: No Longer Just a Dream. 37

Chapter 4: Was I Wrong?. 43

Chapter 5: The Ache of Surrender 53

Chapter 6: Could It Be?. 63

Chapter 7: Miracles Do Still Happen. 77

Part 3: Bringing Selah Home

Chapter 8: Seeing What We Believe. 101

Chapter 9: God's Protective Hand 107

Chapter 10: Getting to Know You 115

Chapter 11: But Why, God?. 137

Chapter 12: His Timing Doesn't Always Seem Fair. .149

Chapter 13: Selah: Chosen, Cherished, Beloved . . . 165

Closing Words 173

Photos 177

INTRODUCTION

In a far-off Bulgarian village, a new mom—young, alone, and without means—walked out of the hospital with empty arms. Her body and emotions exhausted, she had done the only thing she knew to do.

Moments after birth, her daughter had felt her biological mother's touch for the last time. Surrendered, she would spend her first three years in the baby orphanage in Plovdiv and the next two years in the small village orphanage in Narechenski Bani.

In the United States, a young couple blissfully enjoyed the blessings of marriage, work, home, and children. Unaware of all that God would place before them, they looked toward the future with confidence.

Thousands of miles apart, no obvious connection, no human ties—how did these lives come together?

Out of all the billions of people in the world, who knew they would meet? Who planned the events in

SURRENDERED HEARTS

each of their lives that would bring them together for a poignant moment in time? Who could connect that one little girl, halfway around the world, to the one family who had prayed for her for years?

Only God.

The Surrendered Heart Manifesto

I love God with my whole heart. I love how He loves me and relentlessly pursues me. I love how He calls me His own and showers me with His grace while longing to see me walk in my holy purpose.

I believe He is my Savior. Jesus alone is my pathway to heaven, and because of Him and His loving sacrifice, I can experience wholeness, freedom, and joy on this side of the cross (this side of heaven). To experience this to the full, however, I must surrender—not part of me, but all of me. In the face of everything *not* of God, I must surrender my fleshly reactions and respond as He calls. And when I mess up, as I surely will, I will run to Him and let His grace pour over me. I will not stay stuck in the shackles of shame or regret.

I will move forward.

I commit to living a surrendered life. A life of trust. When patience eludes me and I don't want to wait anymore, I will choose to trust God's timing. When the world around me screams injustice and I ache to lash out, I will trust God's infinite wisdom. As chaos swirls around me, tempting me to hypercontrol my world, I will choose instead to respond with balance and trust. When the fears of *what if* threaten to envelop me, I commit instead to the bravery we have when we trust Christ. And finally, when doubt and worry seep through my armor, I commit to trust that my God is bigger than anything I am facing, and somehow—someway—it will all be okay.

Part 1

GOD PREPARES US

For we are God's handiwork,
created in Christ Jesus to do
good works, which God prepared
in advance for us to do.
Ephesians 2:10 niv

Chapter 1

WHY ADOPTION?

Pure and genuine religion in the sight
of God the Father means caring for
orphans and widows in their distress.
James 1:27 NLT

Adoption isn't just about growing families. It's not about rescuing or picking out a child to call your own. It's about God and His unfailing love for us. It's about the fact that you are His—no matter where you are or what your story looks like. It's about miracles, love, and relentless pursuit. And it's about surrender and trust.

I don't know that there ever existed a time when adoption didn't have a place in my heart. Maybe it was the little girl from Korea who became my best friend in kindergarten. Maybe it was my mom who wasn't from the United States and at times still struggled with culture and language. Or maybe it was those haunting images on television of children in need.

I cannot name any specific event that made adoption a part of my life vision. I believe God was at work from the beginning, orchestrating all the events in my life in preparation for what would someday be. He was preparing my heart for the little girl who would break it into a million pieces and teach me to love in a way I'd never experienced before. Love that is stronger, more resilient. Love that is fierce.

> Our adoption story is about embracing God's will and the miracles that happen when we least expect them.

While the adoption process is joyful, it is also painful. Yet there walks God, right into the middle of the grief and brokenness, and He makes a family. Of course, that doesn't erase the grief. Anyone who's experienced it knows it doesn't simply disappear when something good happens. The grief stays—it becomes a part of the new story. It may never fully go away, but somehow, intricately and beautifully, God weaves it into the fabric of a forever family.

For our family, there isn't a story without God. I know that people of all beliefs walk the adoption

WHY ADOPTION?

journey, and some might argue the reality of God, or more specifically, the reality of Jesus. But for us, bringing our Selah home had too many coincidences, birthed too much soul-wrenching love, and wowed us with too many miracles to not point to the God of the universe. And with the chains broken, a child once held captive was freed and claimed as chosen, cherished, and beloved. That, my friends, is the work of Jesus.

Our adoption story is a story of love. The kind that forces you to surrender your will and learn to trust. It is a story about brokenness, grief, patience, determination, and faith. And then it's about embracing God's will and the miracles that happen when we least expect them.

Chapter 2

THE STORY BEGAN
LONG BEFORE WE KNEW

He who began a good work in you
will carry it on to completion until
the day of Christ Jesus.
Philippians 1:6 NIV

As a child, I knew about God. I soaked in the
Bible stories my mother read to me out of
my favorite children's Bible, but still I didn't
know the Word of God—and there's a significant
difference. You see, knowing the stories gives us a few
history lessons and a general outline of who God is.
Knowing the Word of God fills in the missing pieces
and teaches us about His character. It draws us near
and allows us to build a relationship with Him. It
becomes a sort of GPS system, leading us to victory
when we live within His will.

When we only know *about* God, we can't fully
understand who we are in Him. We don't grasp the

true value of our identity as children of God. And without that knowledge, the things of this world can take hold of us far too quickly.

Brokenness is a part of life. We all experience it. We are all affected by it. There is no escaping it. As a child, I didn't know how to protect myself from the brokenness of the world. I didn't know how to put on the armor of God. So I slipped, faded, and fell into places I never wanted to be. Places that perpetuated a vicious cycle of brokenness, of guilt, and of condemnation in my life that would take me years to overcome.

> When we only know *about* God, we can't fully understand who we are in Him. We don't grasp the true value of our identity as children of God. And without that knowledge, the things of this world can take hold of us far too quickly.

If only I had understood all that Jesus did for me as He paid the price for my sin with His own life on the cross, defeating the enemy forever. If only I had understood that my value was not tied to the mistakes I'd made, that His love was for me, despite my

THE STORY BEGAN LONG BEFORE WE KNEW

past. But I didn't, and because of that, I traveled in darkness for a long time.

But God uses darkness too. What I couldn't see then, that I do see now, is how God could take all the ugly—the hurt, the pain, the shame, the sin— and use it for good. It's not that He wanted me to suffer or sin, but suffering is inevitable in this broken world. And because we are human, we cannot achieve perfection. Not even near it. So, yes, we will sin. But if we lean into Him and, in an act of surrender, ask Him to forgive us and make our hearts new, He can and will redeem our messes.

Every broken step I took, God used as preparation for what was to come. With loving care, He weaved together those early broken steps with later, well-chosen ones and created in me the groundwork I needed for surrender. Through them, He prepared me to grieve for the broken and to have a heart for the least of these. He prepared me to believe in the miracle and power of His love.

He gave me a heart to serve children, and I pursued a bachelor's degree in elementary education and then a master's degree in bilingual and multicultural education. I spent my days in the classroom teaching children and the evenings teaching adults.

SURRENDERED HEARTS

After a long and winding road, I finally met the man God had intended for me all along. In June of 2000, Bryan and I were married. Two years later, we had our first child. We knew that parenthood would change our lives forever, but we were not prepared for the depth of that change. I don't think any expectant parents can wrap their minds around the kind of love that is born with our children. I know Bryan and I didn't fully get it until our son, Zachary, was born. The elation and wonder of the life that had grown within me was suddenly multiplied by a love I still can't fully describe. But I know it's a closer version of the kind of love God has for us. For you and for me.

Within a few hours of birth, our little guy started showing signs that something wasn't quite right. Over the next forty-eight hours, we learned that Zachary was sick and would have to remain in the hospital. He would be under close observation by doctors; surgery was inevitable.

Another painful season, yet one of preparation. More time to learn to surrender and trust.

Two years later, we celebrated the blessing of baby number two growing in my belly. But just a few weeks after the initial celebration, complications set in, and I miscarried our baby.

THE STORY BEGAN LONG BEFORE WE KNEW

It didn't make sense. I didn't understand why, and I still don't have that answer. But I do know God used that pain as preparation.

Another pregnancy brought us our son Landon. Again we experienced that beautiful explosion of love, another marvelous glimpse into the Father's unfailing love for us. My feelings of awe and thankfulness toward my heavenly Father came together there, and all I could think of was how blessed I was that He had so lovingly given me these beautiful boys to call my own here on earth. In those moments—the miracle moment of each child's birth—I grasped the incomparable magnificence of God deeper than I ever had before.

And it was also the moment that Christ birthed in me a deep ache for the children who didn't have a mommy to hold them close or comfort them when they cried. For the children who didn't have a family to call their own.

It's All Preparation

It's funny how God lays out His plan for us. The twists and turns make little sense in the here and now. Yet when we look back, we see how they all fit together as pieces of a complicated yet beautiful puzzle.

Psalm 119:105 (NLT) says, "Your word is a lamp to guide my feet and a light for my path." God gives us precisely enough light to see sometimes only the step ahead, but He leaves uncovered the biggest of surprises and sometimes the most difficult of seasons. Those steps are never wasted though. God wisely uses them as preparation for what lies ahead.

A longing within me for something more had always endured—for *someone* more—as though a seat at the table were empty. Because of my age and complications with pregnancy, I knew we wouldn't add to our family biologically. And honestly, with a heart already broken for the millions of children in need of families, I couldn't find the justification for more biological children—*for us*. I only knew that if Bryan and I were meant to have more children, it would be through adoption.

> A longing within me for something more had always endured—for *someone* more—as though a seat at the table were empty.

The steps of my life led me into work and ministry with children coming from hard places. I changed from a comfortable upper-class-neighborhood teaching job to a school serving and loving the children and families from an

THE STORY BEGAN LONG BEFORE WE KNEW

impoverished neighborhood. I was drawn in deeply by these children and felt an unrelenting ache for each one who passed through my classroom doors. Most of these children were not orphans, but they were children living without the day-to-day necessities of food, shelter, and sadly, love. Many lived a reality of abuse and neglect.

I found myself daily looking into the eyes of pain, and my heart was forever broken. Through the wrong I witnessed, God filled my heart with a compassion that would lead me to use all my steps of preparation for good. Luke 7:13 (NLT) teaches us that Jesus was filled with compassion for others. When He came face to face one day with a broken woman who had just lost her son, "His heart overflowed with compassion. 'Don't cry!' he said." And then He raised her son from the dead.

I knew I wanted to do something to help hurting children. Jesus had filled me with a growing compassion, and I *needed* to do something about it.

Some Friends Are Jesus with Skin On

I was part of the praise team at our church, and one evening at practice we met the latest addition to our team—our new director. I sensed something

SURRENDERED HEARTS

different about Coleen right away. Her passion for worship was obvious, but not nearly as much as her love for Jesus.

We quickly became friends and found that our families clicked as well. She was my soul sister. A new level of faith began for me. A fire grew within me, and the chains that had held me back began to break.

At the time, Coleen and her family were in the beginning stages of the adoption process. Their story was a testimony to us as we watched the miracle of adoption take place. I watched and listened and tried to be there as this family went through all the ups and downs of adoption. Then referral day arrived. What a miracle it was! The moment I saw their beautiful little girl's photo, I knew she had been handpicked to be a part of that family.

My friend traveled to meet her child, and I cried almost daily as I read the blog entries detailing the days that led up to her finally getting to hold her daughter in her arms and tell her how much she loved her. I cried in the airport as I saw the tears in her daddy's eyes. I watched him completely melt as he held his daughter for the first time. And since then? There have been many more tears of celebration for this child and this family. Tears and laughter for a

THE STORY BEGAN LONG BEFORE WE KNEW

little girl who has flourished beyond words, whose sparkling eyes befit the princess she is. A princess to her family that loves her to the moon and back and to the one and only King.

No sign of an orphan girl remains, but a complete transformation to a child absolutely cherished and forever loved. The orphanage doctors had labeled her significantly delayed with special needs, yet Jesus has healed all of that and moved innumerable mountains. His glory has been abundantly displayed within the lives of each member of this precious family.

God was at work in us. He intersected our lives as preparation. As their story unfolded, so did ours. As their love for their daughter birthed, grew, and flourished, so did the call to adopt in my husband. As much as I knew I wanted to adopt, he didn't. He didn't feel that call. He didn't feel the empty seat at the table. But through this family, and in particular, this little girl, I watched layers of reserve wash away. My husband's heart softened. No, it melted.

Part 2

OUR MIRACLE

IF I WERE YOU, I WOULD APPEAL TO
GOD; I WOULD LAY MY CAUSE BEFORE
HIM. HE PERFORMS WONDERS THAT
CANNOT BE FATHOMED, MIRACLES
THAT CANNOT BE COUNTED.
JOB 5:8—9 NIV

Chapter 3

No Longer Just a Dream

For in this hope we were saved. Now
hope that is seen is not hope. For
who hopes for what he sees? But if
we hope for what we do not see, we
wait for it with patience.

Romans 8:24–25 ESV

As time passed, Bryan and I discussed the possibility of adoption. His concerns were financial. Adoption is an expensive process, and he wanted to be sure we could embark on this journey without putting our family at risk. He worried about all the things a good father worries about. On top of that, he is an accountant by trade, so Excel sheets are a part of the package.

During that time, we bought a new house, planning to sell the previous one once we had moved. However, the market bottomed out, and selling

SURRENDERED HEARTS

became a losing battle. We decided to rent the home but found that more of a management fiasco than a lucrative investment. The burden of the debt with the house held him back. All I could do was pray.

And God moved.

The renters had a job change and needed to move. We did a fast two-week overhaul and got it on the market. Within twenty-four hours, we had a full-price offer. Three weeks later, it closed. The next day, Bryan and I stood in our master bedroom overlooking our backyard, and I said, "Look at all this. God has blessed us with so much—so that we can be a blessing to others."

Then he asked me, "Do you still want to adopt?"

With my heart pounding and eyes wide open in surprise, I smiled and said, "Of course!"

To which I heard, "Well, let's get this started then."

In a matter of one month, we went from hardly any talk of adoption, because of a financial situation that didn't seem to have a resolution, to starting the process of bringing our little girl home forever. God was moving mountains, and I couldn't have been more excited.

No Longer Just a Dream

By November of 2008, we were convinced that God was leading us to Bulgaria and to where the little girl He had handpicked for us was waiting. In January of 2009, we decided to use All God's Children International as our adoption agency. We completed both the pre-application and official application the next month.

Urgency Challenges Our Desire to Wait Well

As each day passed, I felt a growing sense of urgency. Maybe it was because each day brought us a bit closer and made it all seem a touch more tangible. Or maybe it was because I believed that our Selah (the name we had chosen for her) had already been born. We had decided to adopt a child between the ages of zero and three years, so it was probable she was already born and waiting.

We knew God was moving in our hearts, and we had the luxury of information. But our little girl didn't. Yet we trusted that somehow God was moving and preparing her heart for the day we could wrap our arms around her and love her forever.

We began praying for her every day. We prayed the Lord would comfort her and fill her with a peace and joy that could come from Him alone. We prayed

SURRENDERED HEARTS

for her to have an unnatural assurance that she would have a forever family and that somehow she would feel the love coming from our hearts, halfway around the world. We prayed that whoever was caring for her would handle her with gentleness and love and would, to the best of their ability, work to meet her needs. We prayed that her birth mother had loved her with all that she had and that she'd found comfort in the Lord, even in her decision to leave her child at an orphanage.

A Season of Preparation Involves a Lot of Work

My daily reality was a never-ending paper chase. Oh my word! I learned a plethora of new initialisms: NBC, MOJ, NGO, USCIS—just to name a few. We filled out forms, met with doctors, sought approvals, submitted to fingerprinting several times, took adoption courses, wrote reams of adoption-related reports, attended interviews, completed a home study, and made countless trips to the office of Arizona's secretary of state to obtain the necessary apostille for every paper that would make its way to Bulgaria. An *apostille* is an international notary seal obtained by first locally notarizing a document and then presenting it

No Longer Just a Dream

in person to the office of the secretary of state for the international one.

We worked with wonderful people from All God's Children and with our local agency. There were days when we were able to complete the paperwork effortlessly. And there were days I wanted to pull my hair out.

> I had no idea how well versed I would become at patient endurance, steadfast faith, and the absolute surrender of my own ideals. Nor did I know how much I would learn about the great art of waiting.

But this was only the beginning of a long season of preparation for us. God had a plan, and as much as we worked to be prepared, educated, and aware, we were oblivious to what was ahead.

I had no idea how well versed I would become at patient endurance, steadfast faith, and the absolute surrender of my own ideals. Nor did I know how much I would learn about the great art of waiting.

SURRENDERED HEARTS

I know what I'm doing. I have it all planned out—plans to take care of you, not abandon you, plans to give you the future you hope for. When you call on me, when you come and pray to me, I'll listen. When you come looking for me, you'll find me.... I'll make sure you won't be disappointed.

—Jeremiah 29:11–14 MSG

Chapter 4

WAS I WRONG?

Patient endurance is what you need
now, so that you will continue to do
God's will. Then you will receive all
that he has promised.
Hebrews 10:36 NLT

Control and trust do not exist simultaneously. Life is a series of taking control of the situations we can and letting go of what we cannot. It's a fine line we walk between the two, and too often we march boldly across the line into what we know is not ours to manage. Yet we fight on, determined to be in control, succeeding only in stressing ourselves out and causing heartache for ourselves and those around us.

From my own experience, I've learned that the less trust I have, the more control I try to exert. When my trust disappears, I start feeling the tension building in my jaw, spreading down my neck and into my shoulders. Then headaches appear and anxiety builds.

I was in that place in our adoption journey. I was on top of every piece of paperwork. Organization is key to navigating the legalities and paperwork required in adoption, but even that will not ensure that everything goes smoothly. The Lord was continuing to break me of my control tendencies and lead me out where I wasn't nearly as comfortable. To surrender. To trust.

> God's plan is rightfully that: *His plan. Not mine.* And that's a tough one for all of us, isn't it?

God's plan is rightfully that: *His plan. Not mine.* And that's a tough one for all of us, isn't it?

Moments That Take Our Breath Away

One morning in January of 2010, I sat down to catch up on my email. The boys were safely off to school, and the house was quiet. Because we were waiting for our referral from the adoption agency, email was the first thing I checked every day. We'd been told the referral might not arrive for possibly another year, but a girl could hope, right?

Was I Wrong?

An email from All God's Children awaited me. It was their typical monthly update, including a small list of children noted as having special needs; those adoptions could be expedited. Finding families willing to adopt children with special needs is more difficult than finding families for healthy children. Therefore, agencies take extra initiative to find families for them.

Bryan and I had determined that we were not willing to step into a special-needs adoption. I wish I could say we went into this with more bravery, but we didn't. We didn't believe we were equipped and didn't sense God pointing us in that direction at that time. So when All God's Children sent out these emails, I scanned the faces and prayed for each child to find their forever family. But I never expected to find the daughter God had handpicked for us on that list.

That morning, however, as I opened my email, a toddler—with brown sparkly eyes and little black ringlets falling around her beautiful face—grabbed hold of me. My heart opened wider than it ever had before. It was a different kind of open, one that showed me yet another facet of God. How He loves us and how He grows the heart of a mother. I hadn't even met this child, but I loved her. My hands shook,

SURRENDERED HEARTS

and—friend, I know it sounds silly, but—I wept. I knew that I knew that I *knew* I had seen my daughter for the first time. And I instantly knew that God grows a child in our hearts as unmistakably as He does in our wombs.

Yet the control side of me worried. What were her special needs? We had agreed to consider only minor needs or none at all. Would Bryan agree? Would he sense what I was sensing? Would he realize that the precious princess in the picture was our daughter?

I opened the email attachments eager to find more details. She was three years and seven months old. By the time we would bring her home, she would most likely be four years old.

> I instantly knew that God grows a child in our hearts as unmistakably as He does in our wombs.

That was slightly older than we'd planned and closer to our son Landon's age than we'd hoped. I continued to read the medicals, and much to my relief, her needs were a speech delay, a heart murmur, and flat feet. *Flat feet?* Really? That's a special need? A speech delay in my world of teaching and connections was not a deal breaker whatsoever, and most heart murmurs were harmless.

WAS I WRONG?

I wanted to call Bryan immediately, but I knew I needed to do this the right way. He's a wonderful man—but stubborn. Strong-arming or surprising him had never been a productive strategy. I waited for what felt like forever, but that evening, after the boys were in bed for the night, I said, "I want you to look at something, Bryan. But you have to promise me not to say one single word until you have looked and read the whole thing. No quick judgments."

With a roll of his eyes, he promised. I opened the email and handed him my computer. The dark brown eyes sparkled right out of that page. I watched my husband, and I saw the reaction I'd been hoping for. He's not an emotional kind of guy, so when his Adam's apple began bobbing and I saw the tears threatening, I knew the Holy Spirit was at work. "Look at her, honey! Her name is Gergana. Those eyes—that hair. She's the vision of the daughter God gave me long ago. I know it says special needs. But, flat feet? Is that really a special need? I can handle speech issues. And usually heart murmurs are not cause for big concern."

We called our agency first thing in the morning. Immediately, we had more paperwork to complete, some consultations, and then a wait for the Bulgarian

SURRENDERED HEARTS

government's decision. Our caseworker assured us these were mere formalities. There was no reason our family wouldn't be approved for this child. The only obstacle would be if multiple families requested to adopt her, which didn't happen often. However, we wouldn't know that in advance of the MOJ (Ministry of Justice) meeting. Our caseworker counseled me to guard my heart. I understood the wisdom behind her counsel, but I also knew what the Holy Spirit had done in me.

I was *meant* to hold this little one in my arms and call her *my daughter*.

The morning of the meeting arrived. It had only been a couple of weeks since we'd first seen her face in that photo. We were all beyond excited. The boys didn't want to go to school; they wanted to wait for the call too. They'd fallen equally in love with the little girl in the picture and couldn't wait to celebrate. Our faith as a family had grown over the process, as had our awe of God. The conviction we all sensed about this child felt like a miracle. What a gift it was to know beyond the shadow of doubt in only one moment of time.

Then my phone rang. By the caller ID, I knew it was our caseworker. The excitement was bubbling. I could hardly keep from giggling.

But the voice on the other end wasn't excited like I'd expected.

The answer was no. She wouldn't be a Schumaker after all. The following is my personal blog entry on that devastating day.

Sunday, January 24, 2010—Not Us

Our news was not what we wanted to hear. The little girl to whom we have all given our hearts has been given to another family.

I praise God that her life will still begin anew, and she will be loved and cherished, but it would be a lie to say that my heart is not broken.

I don't understand why God made my heart respond to her in such a way and allowed me to fall deeply in love with her. I don't understand how our family, even our sweet boys, could see her as the perfect fit. I don't know why it felt completely right. But for some reason, the MOJ decided on another family. I must believe God's hand was in that and that He's doing what's best for her and for us. He sees the bigger picture, and I am thankful to Him for that, but it has left an ache in my heart . . . a big one. I don't like this side to the emotional roller coaster of adoption.

> "For My thoughts are not your thoughts,
> Nor are your ways My ways," declares the
> Lord. "For as the heavens are higher than
> the earth, So are My ways higher than
> your ways And My thoughts higher than
> your thoughts."
>
> —Isaiah 55:8–9 AMP

The Moments That Break Us into a Million Pieces

How could I have been this profoundly wrong? How could I have misunderstood what I thought to be the clearest thing God had *ever* communicated to me?

WAS I WRONG?

The next few months were a season of frustration that left me unable to verbally express my thoughts and feelings. After all, how was I to explain this overwhelming

> Just as you love a baby growing in your womb, you can love a child halfway round the world. It doesn't matter how—it just matters who.

grief for a child I had not met, of whom I had seen only a couple pictures and viewed approximately seven minutes of video? How could I explain that to the people in my life who had not experienced what I had?

God-things often don't make sense in the flesh. When someone's heart is open to the movement of God, they see Him in it. But if their minds are closed, His workings don't reverberate with them. Instead they write off those things as strange. It's like that with adoption.

If you've been called to adopt, you get it. It doesn't matter if you know it's in the plans for someday or if you are currently walking the journey. When your heart is moved, you know there is no turning back; you know the power of love. The love God births inside you makes hardly any sense to someone not

SURRENDERED HEARTS

involved. Just as you love a baby growing in your womb, you can love a child halfway around the world. It doesn't matter how—it just matters who.

People often ask how we knew we wanted to adopt. They ask how we knew where in the world to look for our child. And they ask us how we knew we could love an adopted child as much as we do our birth children.

I can't explain it well. But I can promise—*you will know*! God doesn't hide His plan from us. He may not reveal every step right from the beginning as far as the who, where, or when, but the details are all in His hands.

For me, the knowing came through the peace I found. Peace will not settle over your soul until you follow the call. As you begin to follow, He opens and shuts doors to show you where to look. And then, as you continue in obedience, patience, and trust, He reveals exactly who He has for you.

Eventually, you find yourself looking into the eyes of the one child out of millions whom God has chosen uniquely for you. *And you simply know.*

Chapter 5

THE ACHE OF SURRENDER

> O Lord, you are my lamp. The
> Lord lights up my darkness. In your
> strength I can crush an army; with
> my God I can scale any wall.
> 2 Samuel 22:29–30 NLT

Grief is complicated. Although there are similar stages through which we all pass, the process is unique to each individual. Often we think of grief only in relation to the loss of a loved one. But grief is also found within the tender parts of hidden loss—the losses those around us may never notice or even recognize as such.

It's found below the surface of life events like divorce, loss of employment, or an unmet goal or dream. We find it in miscarriage, infertility, adoption, and even when a young woman makes the decision to abort. This list is only a beginning. Grief lives hand in hand with our existence here on earth. It also lives hand in hand with joy. We don't have much of one without the other. Yet as a society, we don't necessarily recognize these places of loss. I know that for those who haven't adopted, understanding the grief I experienced after losing the child I'd firmly believed was ours is difficult.

Honestly, a year earlier I wouldn't have understood it either. God gives us a mommy's love whether that child grows within our wombs or within our hearts. Whether we fall in love at our child's first breath of air or at the first glimpse of her photo, it is a miracle. This love can only come from something vastly larger than ourselves. In fact, it could only come from the One who created love. This vivid example mirrors how God adopts us into His family the moment we ask Him to be the Lord of our lives. We become part of His treasured family, and His love is absolutely, without a doubt, unfailing and unwavering.

Grudges Don't Set Us Free

But there I was, without even realizing it, holding the biggest grudge against Him. And for what? For this miracle of love given by Him as a gift. And now I was mad that He had given that love to me, because it left me hurting.

THE ACHE OF SURRENDER

I know it sounds a bit ignorant to say I didn't realize I was holding that grudge, but I can promise you I was telling myself all the right things straight from the Word of God. Any of my girlfriends would verify that. I was doing grief with grace. I seemed to be coping well. I listened to godly counsel and teaching and nodded my head in agreement to all of it because I *knew* it was right. But where it mattered most, I didn't get it. My heart simply wasn't feeling it.

Grudge-holding does nothing more than keep us stuck. It breeds bitterness and distances us, not only from the one we resent, but from the most rewarding parts of life. I hid the distance well—even from myself. I didn't feel the presence of the Holy Spirit, but I convinced myself it certainly wasn't because I was holding a grudge. That is where religion and relationship are two different things.

I was doing what my religion had taught me—going to church, reading my Bible, listening to worship music, praying. Those were all great things to do, but there was more, and I was missing it. I had lost heart, and then I lost relationship. My prayers became mere religious talk. I wasn't being real with God. I was not being honest enough with Him to tell

55

Him I was mad. After all, good girls don't get mad at God, right?

But the truth of the matter was that I had put distance between us, and before healing could begin I had to let Him back into my heart. My relationship with Him had become lukewarm, and lukewarm might get me by, but it surely wasn't going to release the chains of grief, disappointment, and anger that were holding me captive. It would also not get me to a place of freedom and joy once again.

Getting Real with God Matters

One weekend, almost five and a half months after our rejection, I had a whole twenty-four hours completely to myself. I spent those hours in prayer, *real prayer*, facing what I had not yet faced. God knew of my anger toward Him. He knew all that I was harboring in my heart. But I needed to face it and be authentic with Him. Real relationship doesn't happen without authenticity.

Friend, it turns out I was mad at Him for a whole lot more than our adoption upset. We get good at stuffing our feelings, at living in denial, at hoping somehow whatever it is will entirely go away. Only it doesn't go away. We stuff ourselves until we burst.

THE ACHE OF SURRENDER

And burst I did—just Jesus, me, and all the emotions I'd stuffed for far too long.

I ranted about how He'd allowed me to sense such a powerful Holy Spirit conviction and then He unmistakably took her away. I blamed Him for my broken heart. I argued that I knew His Word, that He knows best, but it surely didn't seem that way right now because there could not be a family better for her than ours. I raged about the standstill in the Bulgarian adoption process, about the recent tragic losses of some special people in our lives, and about some chronic medical issues I was dealing with. I let it *all* pour out. And once it started, it kept coming.

It was like the backyard water hose. You know when it gets that kink in it that stops the water flow? The water can be turned on full force at the source, but with a kink in the line, nothing comes out the other end. When the integrity of the line is restored, the water bursts through. That was me. Things I didn't even know were bothering me rushed out. As I poured out the pain, the anger, and the hurt to Him, I felt His reassuring comfort that said, *It's okay.*

He loves it when we share with Him from the deepest places of our souls. He loves authenticity. Yes, He already knows it all, but when we're willing to share it, that means we're being real with Him. We're engaging in relationship with Him, just as He desires. The truest and deepest relationships we have here on earth are with those we share the most. They're with the friends we trust, the ones who love us exactly as we are. That's the kind of relationship God wants to have with us.

God reassured me that night and taught me that my trust in Him was made evident by my prayer-filled confessions. I had finally come to a point of trust and surrender. I was finally at a place where I could let Him heal my ache and work all things out in *His* time.

> When we enter true relationship with the Father, the scales fall away from our eyes and the weight of bitterness melts away. It is then, as we trust enough to surrender, that we find real relationship. It is then, through our moments of prayer, worship, and praise, that we find the hope, peace, and joy we were longing for.

Until this point, I had been faking it. And faking it didn't work. I had been praying polite prayers—the kind of conversation you have with a stranger, not with a trusted confidant and best friend. I had

THE ACHE OF SURRENDER

politely asked God to give me strength, wisdom, and patience. I'd asked Him to give me those things as though I were requesting it from a stranger at a fast-food chain. You see, because of my grudge, I couldn't get close enough to Him to ask for what I really needed. I wanted Him to hand over the power without walking with Him. I didn't want to praise Him in the storm. I wanted what I wanted without having to get too close.

But if He would have given me those things, I would have let them go to waste because I am nothing without Him. What I needed to ask was, "Lord, please *be* my strength, my wisdom, my patience, my everything!" God *wants* to be our strength. He wants to fill us with the power of the Holy Spirit, but we can't receive that power unless we lay everything before Him in a way that is honest and raw. Until we surrender.

When we enter true relationship with the Father, the scales fall away from our eyes and the weight of bitterness melts away. It is then, as we trust enough to surrender, that we find real relationship. It is then, through our moments of prayer, worship, and praise, that we find the hope, peace, and joy we were longing for.

And just maybe it's what God was waiting for all along. Maybe that's what it takes to move into the next chapter of life. I know it was for me.

My Encouragement:
O Lord, you are my lamp. The Lord lights up my darkness. In your strength I can crush an army; with my God I can scale any wall. God's way is perfect. All the Lord's promises prove true. He is a shield for all who look to him for protection. For who is God except the Lord? Who but our God is a solid rock? God is my strong fortress, and he makes my way perfect. He makes me as surefooted as a deer, enabling me to stand on mountain heights. He trains my hands for battle; he strengthens my arm to draw a bronze bow. You have given me your shield of victory; your help has made me great. You have made a wide path for my feet to keep them from slipping. —2 Samuel 22:29–37 NLT

My Prayer:
Lord, please be my strength in weakness, my wisdom in ignorance, my patience in frustra-

THE ACHE OF SURRENDER

tion, my love in anger. Lord, I ask for Your Holy Spirit to permeate my being, to be all that I am not. When the surrender aches, I ask You to propel me forward in trust, reminding me that You will not fail me. I thank You for being my solid rock—my strong fortress. Thank You for loving me when I'm not that loveable. In Your perfect name I pray. Amen.

Chapter 6

COULD IT BE?

He alone is your God, the only one
who is worthy of your praise, the one
who has done these mighty miracles
that you have seen with your own eyes.
Deuteronomy 10:21 NLT

Peace was a welcome breath of life-giving air.
It's amazing what shedding the heavy burden of grudge-bearing can do for the soul.
Through surrender, my heart, soul, and mind had
finally aligned. I understood the heart of adoption
better. I understood what love was a little more. And
I could finally say, *Thank You, Lord, for allowing me
this glimpse into Your truth.*

Adoption is a privilege. It's a step into the unknown, and it's not for those who are not willing to
strengthen the warrior within. God gave me the opportunity to love a young girl in a way that I couldn't
wrap my head around. I thought the love I felt had

come only because He'd said she was mine. But I'd forgotten that she was His first. His ways are beyond my understanding. They are greater than anything I am capable of conjuring. In fact, He tells me that in Isaiah 55:8–9 (ESV):

> My thoughts are not your thoughts, neither are your ways my ways, declares the Lord. For as the heavens are higher than the earth, so are my ways higher than your ways and my thoughts than your thoughts.

For this reason, if He placed her in my heart yet gave her to another family, then I must believe that prayer was His request of me. Peace would follow when I walked God's journey instead of my own. His gift to me was allowing me to be her prayer warrior for all the days of my life. No matter when our adoption happened—sooner, later, or not at all—I was convinced I could rest in the peace that comes with the trust I had gained. I had given back what was originally His, and I had

> Peace would follow when I walked God's journey instead of my own.

stopped trying to own something that was never meant to be mine.

I wanted to trust that gift and surrender my longing for more, so I prayed constantly. I prayed for her family to know and love the Lord. I asked that she would be loved unconditionally and that God would restore all her brokenness and sorrow. And I prayed for her birth mother and whatever she was facing.

Beauty out of the Surrender

Within a couple of weeks of finding this peace, I remembered that I had registered for a Bulgarian adoption chat group. (This was before Facebook groups existed.) I had joined the group the same month I'd seen Gergana's photo, but in the months that followed after losing her, I'd lost all desire to read about the adoptions of others. That was part of my grief process and part of the grudge I'd been nursing. Now, with my newfound peace, I was ready to engage again. I was curious about any new developments in the adoption world.

When I logged in, I found almost six hundred emails waiting my attention. Should I delete them all and start over fresh? I didn't have time to go through all of them. Deleting them would make more sense.

But something stopped me from purging them all at once.

Instead, I started with the oldest, deleting those with completely unrelated content, but diligently following the threads to which I had a personal connection. Overall, something had happened within the group. It's a common thing in any support group—we easily get stuck in the junk and forget the joy of Jesus. It's good to ask questions, share information, and vent in a safe place. Yet it's important not to get stuck in the negative—in the junk.

People were frustrated with timelines going way beyond what had been communicated. They were frustrated with paperwork, laws, rules, and mistakes. And I couldn't blame them. Adoption is a challenging journey with laws intended to protect. Yet those very laws often seem to cause good people and children more trouble and delay. Instead of protecting, they hurt. The criminals still manage to find their way through the system, but people of pure heart struggle to save a child.

I was determined, though, as I worked my way through the months of communications, to stay positive and keep my joy, because I was committed to living out my newfound gift of peace. Through all the writings, the voice of one woman stood out, Yvonne. I was drawn to her, wanting to know the details of her story. Her words spoke to my heart in an encouraging way. She was a voice of reason in a turbulent sea of frustration.

In the six months I had been absent from the group, Yvonne had gone from receiving her child referral, to the first visit with her child, and to the second trip of bringing her daughter home. I even got glimpses into her first few weeks of life at home. Her posts were a joy to read and a reassurance of what the heart of adoption is all about. It took me over a week to catch up, but as soon as I did, I had an unmistakable inclination to send her an email.

Back then, however, I was merely a lurker. Social media wasn't what it is today. In fact, as far as I was concerned, it still bordered on terrifying. The impulse to message her was something new for me.

My message was simple. I offered congratulations for her recent adoption and a word of gratitude for her encouragement, positive comments, and voice of reason.

I didn't expect a reply. I knew she was home, settling into a new normal with her daughter. My message didn't require a response. It was merely a shout-out. But to my surprise, she not only responded with gratitude, but she asked me questions about our adoption process.

We began corresponding by email every few days, and after several weeks I shared with her a few of the details surrounding our failed attempt at adoption. I described how passionately our family had fallen in love with "our" little girl, and I told her about our rejection and the tremendous grief that had followed.

Bulgaria has strict rules about sharing public information about any of their children in the orphanages, and saying too much to the wrong person or in a public setting could jeopardize your ability to adopt from their country. It's not safe to share details like the names of children, orphanages, directors, or really, any other specific information. Hence, before I could share any details, this woman had to earn my wholehearted trust.

Over time, she did earn that trust, and as she asked more questions, I laid out all the details of the child who had stolen my heart—the one I had given back to God in surrender and trust. But when I did so, I received a strange email from my new friend.

Yvonne's message was urgent, expressing her desire for me to meet Monica, a friend of hers from

COULD IT BE?

Hawaii. She explained that our stories were similar and that we would have a lot to share with each other. She asked if she could pass along my email address. I agreed.

God was at work putting together the pieces of our story. He could have done it the easy way, without the heartache and complications. He is able.

> He was showing us beyond any doubt that He had handpicked the child He would give us. Not by chance. Not by mistake. Not by me. She was chosen, planned before the beginning of time to be a Schumaker.

But without the complications and the heartache, we don't notice Him. In our pride, we attribute smooth events to our own abilities. We become blind to His majesty and take matters into our own hands, claiming the victory as ours. For us, He was working the miraculous. He was showing us beyond any doubt that He had handpicked the child He would give us. Not by chance. Not by mistake. Not by me. She was chosen, planned before the beginning of time to be a Schumaker.

Yvonne hadn't revealed much at all about the woman she wanted me to meet, but something

69

stirred within my soul telling me she was important to our adoption journey. The connecting email arrived the next day. I smiled, loving the idea of getting to know this woman, yet a bit apprehensive because, after all, I had barely surrendered this whole process. I didn't want the temptation of pulling it back into my possession. I needed the peace I'd found, and I felt good in it. There was no sense of urgency on my part to reengage.

Rising Bravely from the Ashes of Our Pain

Several days later, I received a heartfelt email from Monica. With tears in my eyes, I read of her painful adoption journey. She had gone through an extraordinarily difficult series of events, facing every hurdle imaginable. She'd started adoption proceedings in several countries, only to have each of them shut down their adoption programs. Then she lost not one, but three children to other families in the referral process. She had even lost a child in the same way we had—and in Bulgaria.

In her situation, the girl from Bulgaria whom Monica had hoped to adopt was given to another family. However, only a few weeks later, she received a phone call reversing the decision and giving her the

COULD IT BE?

referral. She was beyond excited at the turn of events because she, too, had felt that this child was meant to be hers.

Monica quickly completed the paperwork, and before she knew it, she was packing for that first journey to meet who she believed to be her daughter. With her heart full of anticipation, she made the long trip to a tiny Bulgarian orphanage tucked away in the mountains near the Greek border. But what happened during her week there wasn't at all what she had anticipated.

What Monica had hoped to happen in those moments together, didn't. This little girl didn't seem to connect or bond with her in any special way. Then when she sought answers to questions from the orphanage director, she ran into dead ends and silence. This child had delays that would mean more therapy and time than she believed she could provide as a single mother working full time. In the deepest part of her soul, she knew this child was not meant to be hers. With her heart breaking and filled with the grief of another lost dream, she talked with her translator and agency representative in hopes of resolving her fears. But in the end, she knew what she needed to do. She would have to send an official letter to decline this referral.

My heart ached for Monica and all the pain she had experienced. I also admired her courage and resiliency. I could not imagine losing a child to another family, then getting her back again, only to discover the child was *not* meant to be mine. The amount of grief accumulated on that emotional roller coaster had to be enormous. And it had to be confusing. How brave of her to follow what she knew to be true instead of going ahead and ignoring the voice telling her the situation was not correct.

> I had surrendered my desire for that little girl to be mine again. I had given her back to the One who had created her and would care for her. I was at peace with the gift of being her forever prayer warrior.

I wondered if I would have had that same courage. Or would I have decided I'd come too far to walk away? Monica had the courage to do the right thing. She listened to that voice inside. She acknowledged her limits and honored who she was created to be. She released that child, but she did not give up after that. She continued to wait for the child meant to be hers.

COULD IT BE?

As I replied to Monica, I prayed. I prayed for her heart that must have been fragile. I prayed for the resiliency of her spirit and for God to bring the child into her life who was meant to be hers. I shared with her our heartbreaking story and explained how the experience had sent my emotions into turmoil. I couldn't fathom the depth of her emotions after all she had weathered.

The email I received in response took my breath away. The memory is vivid even today.

Remember, I had surrendered my desire for that little girl to be mine again. I had given her back to the One who had created her and would care for her. I was at peace with the gift of being her forever prayer warrior.

But in Monica's email, she explained that I had not read the earlier message quite correctly. There were places I was supposed to read between the lines. We were both aware that breaking country adoption rules could remove us from the process, and we feared revealing too much. Wanting desperately to communicate clearly, but awkwardly aware of the need for caution, my spirit knew that more to this story was unfolding.

SURRENDERED HEARTS

I was a mess, fluctuating between my jaw dropping and my heart pounding and then dismissing any possibilities. Where exactly was I supposed to read between the lines? I didn't know.

Two things surfaced in my thought process. One, sometimes I live in a bubble, because it's quite comfortable there. And two, maybe this sweet lady really wasn't as sweet as I thought she was. Maybe she was actually wacky, or worse yet, evil. It wasn't the soundest thought, but I couldn't get past it. What if this was the enemy's way of tempting me? I wasn't going to allow it.

But I responded with another email: "I am truly confused. I know sometimes I live in the safety of a bubble, but where should I have read between the lines?"

Her response?

"The little girl I thought was mine, whom I visited in Bulgaria not long ago, I referred to as *Gigi*. That is not her real name. I used the name because her real name has two G's in it."

The child I had surrendered back to God—whom I still loved with my whole heart—her name was Gergana. Was this woman trying to tell me that the two were actually the same little girl? Again, my first

COULD IT BE?

reaction was disbelief. I'd been told repeatedly that our Gergana had been adopted by an Italian family. I had asked my caseworker several times if anything in her status had changed, because we still wanted her. My caseworker knew how much we loved her; she had been heartbroken with us. She would have told us if an American had gotten the referral.

This just could not be true.

But, there were all these coincidences to account for. So many odd connections—me in Arizona, using an agency in Oregon, communicating with an orphanage in Bulgaria. And then, through a chat group of more than seven hundred families, I had noticed the posts of one woman in Ohio—a woman to whom I had uncharacteristically sent a private email because her posts spoke to my heart. And she knew another woman—in Hawaii, of all places—whose story coincided with mine. And *that* woman might possibly have just declined the referral of *our* Gergana, *which would mean she was still available for adoption!*

Either Monica was intentionally trying to hurt us, or it had to be a different girl who happened to have the same name and age.

Or—could it be? Could God be orchestrating the unbelievable?

Chapter 7

MIRACLES DO STILL HAPPEN

> Look at the nations and watch—and
> be utterly amazed. For I am going to
> do something in your days that you
> would not believe, even if you were told.
> Habakkuk 1:5 NIV

Sometimes hope is scary. Hoping for the impossible feels a lot like letting go. It's giving your heart a chance to hurt again. But it's also giving your faith a chance to point to a God who is bigger than your mountains.

Could It Be?

After that email conversation, that's exactly how I felt. Scared. I had surrendered my little girl; I had given her back to God. Picking up hope again for what seemed impossible felt risky, as though I were letting my guard down and leaving myself emotionally vulnerable. But I also felt the exhilaration that hope brings. One minute I wanted to jump for joy, and the next I wanted to dive into a quart of my favorite ice cream. I had to fervently seek God's peace. Only with Him would calm, cool, and collected prevail over anxiety and quarts of ice cream.

God has a way of giving us exactly what and who we need in life. Sometimes the uniqueness of that *who* can drive us mad. Yet when it matters, often the very attribute that drives us mad is what brings the balance we need. And that's my husband—rock solid, steady. Almost always in control of his emotions (unless he is watching KU basketball). He faces life with logic rather than emotions. Sometimes that logic frustrates me, but most of the time it's what I need to balance my emotions.

So, with rock steady in place, he listened to my recounting of the emails. The more animated I became, the more expressionless he became. I was frustrated. Maybe it was me looking for the confirmation to go ahead and hope; I'm not sure. But I know I wanted more.

My husband was afraid for me. Afraid to lose me to sadness again. Afraid I would lose the gains I'd made and take our girl back from Jesus. He was relieved I had surrendered and found peace, and he didn't want to encourage me in any direction of thinking that this Gergana could legitimately be our daughter. For months, he had helplessly watched my tears and heard my relentless insistence that the telephone would ring and they would tell us she *was* meant to be ours. He did not want to chance any of that hurt coming back for me; therefore, he gave me nothing—*even after I read him that last email.* Oh, his immense ability for self-discipline!

But for him, settling on an alternative explanation for these coincidences was the safest place to rest. We compromised, and I agreed to pursue the situation only as far as I needed to gain clarity. I promised not to get ahead of myself, and I reassured him of my peace, no matter the results of my search.

I emailed Monica again, and then the boys and I headed to our cabin in northern Arizona. It had been damaged in a recent storm, and there was enough work to be done there to keep me from hyperventilating over the evolving situation.

That evening at the cabin, I received Monica's next email, and in it she assured me that her Gergana was my Gergana. I had firmly voiced my concern that this little girl had to be a different child, but she did not waver. She explained that, *without a doubt*, she knew the two girls were one and the same. The child she had released was the very same child we had attempted to adopt. *She was our Selah.*

The content of her message convinced me, and once it did, there was no going back. The Lord was calling, and I needed to follow because, friend, if we don't follow when He calls, we will never find peace. But I also needed clarity and direction from the Lord. I needed to hear if this was what He wanted me to do. I needed to feel His blessing and guidance to calm my soul.

I wanted to talk to Bryan, but it was late, and I knew he had to work in the morning. I didn't want to wake him up. I decided to wait until morning, though I was unable to sleep. I spent the night pleading with God for wisdom. Our next steps would affect not only Bryan and me, but also our two sweet boys who had also grieved the loss of the girl whom they thought of as their sister. Should I pursue this further and enter the realm of hope again? Would we have the strength to withstand the disappointment again if the whole story turned out to be false or if

> The Lord was calling, and I needed to follow because, friend, if we don't follow when He calls, we will never find peace.

another family had adopted Gergana in the meantime? I needed to be sure my mind and heart were in alignment with God's will. Pursuing this adoption had to be His will, not my own.

Drawing Closer to Listen to the Author of Our Story

There's a trap into which we often fall. It's the trap of wanting something or someone simply because it's beyond our reach. We push until we get what we want, even if the item is beyond our financial means or the person is not a healthy partner for us. I didn't want this to be the case with our little girl. If God didn't mean for us to be her family, then I needed to let go.

Was I feeling His assurance and was He working a miracle, or was the enemy tempting me?

It occurred to me during that long night that if one or even two other families had declined her referral, it might mean that she was delayed beyond our parenting ability. Again, was she meant to be ours? I prayed, asking for direction from His Word. I opened my Bible and asked God to reveal His will. I asked Him to open wide my eyes, ears, mind, and heart so I could discern what it was that I needed to know.

SURRENDERED HEARTS

God led me to the book of Ezra. It was not a book in the Bible that had ever stood out to me before, and I knew the Spirit was working. I began reading. The book of Ezra is the story of a group of strong, faithful people trying to rebuild the temple of God and restore it to all its former beauty and glory. The people face great opposition each step of the way. They grow weary from the intense oppression, but in these moments of weariness and weakness, God sends prophets with words of encouragement to inspire their continued pursuit of the calling on their lives.

What I read reflected the war waging within me. Overwhelmed by the presence of the Holy Spirit, I realized that, without a doubt, He had guided me exactly where I needed to be. Specifically, God impressed upon me the need to continue with diligence and care; He assured me that our work would prosper in our hands. Here are some of the verses that stood out to me:

> Let it be known to the king that we went into the province of Judah, to the house of the great God. The people are rebuilding it with large stones, and

MIRACLES DO STILL HAPPEN

> placing timbers in the walls. This work is being carried out diligently and is prospering in their hands. —Ezra 5:8 BSB

> And there by the Ahava Canal, I proclaimed a fast, so that we might humble ourselves before our God and ask Him for a safe journey for us and our children, with all our possessions.... So we fasted and petitioned our God about this, and He granted our request. —Ezra 8:21, 23 BSB

The Holy Spirit was at work guiding and directing. I knew exactly what I needed to do. Convicted by the words I had read only a moment before and needing Him to hear my petition, I decided to fast. Turning away a gift from anyone is never wise, so why would I want to turn away a gift presented by the Lord?

Fasting had always intimidated me, but stepping forward in faith is a part of the surrender. It is part of every trust journey. Often, we think of fasting solely in terms of going without food for various lengths of time. But when we think of it in those terms, we can miss out on opportunities to draw closer to the heart of God.

SURRENDERED HEARTS

Fasting is the act of giving up something we need (or are accustomed to having) consistently throughout our day. Whatever that is, giving it up is not easy. Our thoughts and cravings return to it throughout the day. When we fast from it, we remove it from reach. Then, each time we long for it throughout the day, we can remind ourselves to turn to God alone for sustenance, to seek His face rather than that *thing* we crave. Fasting is an act of worship and an expression of personal devotion.

For some of us, that all-important need involves food or drink, whether it's all food or merely one specific kind. For others, it can be technology, social media, or television. Whatever item or activity you choose to abstain from, as you do so, you will be reminded again and again to turn to the Lord for what you need, instead of turning to that vice. And the more we draw closer to God in our need, the more answers we will hear. I thought of Anna in Luke 2:36–37 (NIV):

> There was also a prophet, Anna, the daughter of Penuel, of the tribe of Asher. She was very old; she had lived with her husband seven years after her marriage,

MIRACLES DO STILL HAPPEN

and then was a widow until she was eighty-four. She never left the temple but worshiped night and day, fasting and praying.

Wanting to be like her, I prayed about what my fasting should look like. I was struggling with some health issues, and I was alone with my boys in the middle of virtually nowhere. I needed to be a coherent and safe mommy for them and not worsen the health issues I was dealing with. Going without food until dinner each day was a possibility, but honestly, that would not be difficult for me. I would not be turning to God every moment, because I usually only crave food in the evenings. During daytime hours, I easily forget to eat.

Consequently, I settled on an area where I have the least willpower. I crave a combination of sweet, salty, and crunchy foods. Despite my efforts to get healthier and lose weight, snacks were always my downfall. A stressful moment? A handful of chips would do. Celebrating? Chocolate, of course. This weakness forever frustrates me! I have tried many times to cut out those things and have failed.

SURRENDERED HEARTS

My fast, I decided, would be about eliminating all snacks—sweet, fried, crunchy, or salty. My own willpower had never accomplished it. The only way I could do this was if it were for something bigger than me. Something more important that a few vanity pounds. I knew it would turn me to the Lord in prayer continuously because, embarrassingly, I knew how deep this secret weakness ran.

Sweet sleep was a welcome gift that evening. It came from the peace that settled softly within my spirit. Peace, I have found, is a by-product of surrender and trust.

I woke up to a missed telephone call and message from Monica. In order to get detailed answers, I had sent her my telephone number. I wasn't sure whether she would call or not, but thankfully she had. I sat there in awe of a God who had moved this quickly to bring me answers. Far quicker than I'd dreamed!

> Peace, I have found, is a by-product of surrender and trust.

Bubbling with nervous excitement and intrigue, I dialed the number and waited. No answer. My heart sank, but feeling somewhat like a top-secret spy, I left a careful message.

MIRACLES DO STILL HAPPEN

Then I took the time to update my husband. I still chuckle at his response. Remember when I said earlier that he'd hardly reacted to my anecdotes? Well, that morning he sheepishly said, "Honey, could you tell me the story from the beginning? To be honest, I didn't really listen. I thought maybe you were still trying to make all this into something that it wasn't."

My first reaction was irritation. I think it's a perfectly human reaction to a husband who has tuned you out. Maybe it was the peace God had given me or the wisdom I had asked for, but as quickly as the irritation surfaced, it disappeared. How could I be angry? He had been trying to protect me the best way he knew how.

So I told him the whole saga again—including the developments from the last twenty-four hours. I fully expected him to hold back, to tell me to wait a while. He's not an impulsive person in any way. But his response was precisely the opposite. He urgently told me, "Make the calls. Find out what is going on. If she is available, we are going to apply again. Don't waste any time!"

Wow! I guess there were no questions in his mind.

My plan that morning had been for the boys and me to take the forty-five-minute drive into town for

SURRENDERED HEARTS

lunch and a movie. But between the phone call I needed to make to our caseworker and the one I still needed to have with Monica, I was running out of time. My boys were running low on patience; ergo, my best option was to get them settled in the car with a movie and do my talking on the road. It wasn't ideal, especially since I knew phone service might drop along the drive, but I got us settled into the car. As I prepared to leave, my phone rang. It was Monica.

With headphones securely attached to protect their sweet ears from my conversation, the boys watched their movie. I don't usually depend on technology to entertain my kids, but this time I did. I didn't want to take any chances with their tender hearts, and I wasn't ready for them to know what was going on. I had an hour and a half before they would come out of the movie trance.

The conversation began awkwardly. How could it not? Two virtual strangers. One wondering if the other was, in all reality, a liar. The conversation was heavy, and the importance of it even heavier. I drove for a while but then pulled into a parking lot. I needed to focus. Distraction wasn't good.

Monica shared the whole story. She explained that the Italian family had received Gergana's first referral

MIRACLES DO STILL HAPPEN

but backed out shortly thereafter without making the first trip to visit her. She did not know the reasons behind their decision. However, because Monica had developed a friendship with someone who knew a member of the Ministry of Justice in Bulgaria, she was able to get the referral without Gergana's file being publicly released. The normal full process didn't take place, and other agencies and caseworkers were not notified of Gergana's change in availability. It's one of those things that happens when you deal with governments—especially foreign ones.

Monica had been elated. Her dreams were coming true. I understood the emotions that surged through her heart. She believed, just as I did, that Gergana was meant to be her child. But her agency had not given her as much background information as ours had. We had viewed a few more videos, and we'd seen that her foot probably had more going on than the flat feet her medical report documented. We knew of her speech delay that came from all her years within the orphanage, as well as her other institutional and developmental delays. We felt equipped to handle that which had been made known to us. We still believed God designed this little girl to be a part of our family.

SURRENDERED HEARTS

Poor Monica, however, had not been informed of all these conditions, and when she arrived in Bulgaria, everything changed. As this sweet woman, longing to be a mother, realized the extend of Gergana's delays, her heart broke with the reality of her situation. She would be a single parent. She needed to work full time. How would she get this child all the services she needed to be healthy? How could she keep up?

Something in Monica's soul kept whispering truth. This girl needed a family with a mom who could stay home with her, someone who could run to the different doctor appointments and therapies that would be necessary. She needed siblings who could give her additional attention. She needed a different kind of family to help her become all she was created to be.

In that moment, as Monica talked with me, she felt conviction settle over her. She told me she now knew without a doubt that *we had been Gergana's family all along.*

We ended the call, and I sat there for a moment processing all that had been said. Certain moments we never forget. Some we have to search for amid the not-so-good, if only to keep our hope alive. But other moments are undeniable. That telephone

MIRACLES DO STILL HAPPEN

conversation was precisely that—a life-changing moment. A life-changing conversation. Emotionally charged with Monica's grief over another broken dream and my own still cautious but burgeoning hope, that call held moments of shock, hope, celebration, and even anger.

I was angry that this child still sat waiting for her forever family. Angry that she'd been left alone with less than what she deserved—because of broken rules and poor communication. All those months I couldn't shake the grief. All the tears involved. The time, the questions, and the wonder of *why?* Why had this all happened? Why so complicated?

Yet right there in the middle of the anger, a different and deeper kind of joy blossomed. I think it was the next step in teaching me that God does make all things good for those who love Him. He redeems what the world breaks. He restores what sin takes away.

> I think it was the next step in teaching me that God does make all things good for those who love Him. He redeems what the world breaks. He restores what sin takes away.

But God

I called our caseworker but was able only to leave a message. I waited—again. Through lunch, the movie, and the drive back, I tried my best to lose myself in the moments with my boys. The messy sweetness and laughter of boy life filled my heart as the clock ticked by.

As we pulled into the driveway, the return call I'd been waiting for arrived. The boys ran off to play, so I dove right in.

"I have reason to believe Gergana has not been adopted and is still available."

I can imagine the thoughts that ran through our caseworker's mind as she heard my words. She was a wonderful, godly woman with a great big heart. She'd been concerned about our family and about me, and her response certainly didn't surprise me. It wasn't so much the words as it was the matter-of-fact yet mothering tone she used. Between the lines, I could hear, *Oh no. Lori has finally gone over the edge.*

"Oh, Lori, nooo," she said. "She is *not* available."

The dam broke and words rushed out. "Believe me—I know I sound crazy, but I can assure you that I am not! I've had a series of conversations with

MIRACLES DO STILL HAPPEN

someone who's proven to me that Gergana is available. The Italian adoption fell through. She was given to another family, and they declined the referral after visiting her. The person I spoke with assures me that she's still available—unless someone else has already stepped in to claim her!"

The caseworker paused. Then, processing her shock, she asked several questions—who, when, where? I told her I didn't want to say any names because it was a complicated story and I feared issues with Bulgarian guidelines. It was better I didn't tell her much of anything because then, if someone asked her, she wouldn't be forced into the middle of any situations.

I did explain enough to share the miracle behind it. It was all a God-story. I honestly had not been searching for this information—it had landed randomly in my lap. I shared with her my own shock and doubt at first.

But I also had tough questions to ask. How was it possible for all this to happen without her knowledge? In all her busyness, had she dropped the ball? Had she missed an email or an alert? I didn't think so, but I couldn't help the thoughts.

SURRENDERED HEARTS

She was confused and genuinely disappointed too. She had experienced the ups, downs, and inconsistencies of adoption through her career, but as I was realizing for the first time, much that happens in the world of adoption is not fair. It all comes down to having the right connections.

The situation was proving to me the promise in Romans 8:28 (NLT), that "God causes everything to work together for the good of those who love God and are called according to his purpose for them." Even when evil intervenes, God's work is stronger.

My conversation with the caseworker ended with her promise to call the Bulgarian agency. She would ask them to contact the Bulgarian Ministry of Justice to find out if Gergana was, in fact, still available for adoption.

> Even when evil intervenes, God's work is stronger.

Once again, we waited. But this time I called in the troops, also known as my Jesus girlfriends. I asked them to pray like never before. I couldn't explain the whole story in detail to everyone on the phone, so through text I shocked them with the basics. *Gergana may be available for adoption again*, I wrote. *I need y'all to pray.* And that is one of the blessings of a community of believers. They're willing to

MIRACLES DO STILL HAPPEN

pray even when they don't know all the details. They will drop everything to call out to Jesus.

I called Bryan. As I relayed all that had happened, thankfulness overwhelmed me. He was convinced this child was ours. Once upon a time that wasn't so, but God. . .

Those are my two favorite words: *But God.*

My great God used the injustice, the delays, and the miscommunications to convince my husband that, beyond the shadow of a doubt, we were following Jesus to exactly the right place.

Before our marriage, adoption was not on Bryan's radar. He listened to me talk about it over the years, but he was honest with me. He didn't see it in his future.

But I prayed. I didn't push or coerce or nag. I just prayed.

Adoption is far too important a journey to take without a united front. Our most difficult challenges bring out our most difficult traits. In the trials and emotions of the process, our weakest areas are vulnerably bared to our mates. This is why a significant number of marriages fall apart when troubles come.

Even for us, while we were unified on our decision to adopt, the difficult times challenged our marriage.

95

SURRENDERED HEARTS

Bryan was at a crucial point in his career. His focus was necessarily there. I agreed to handle most everything on my own. He did the parts he was required to, but often not without complaint. I understood—yet sometimes it was tough—and I wanted him to be more involved. I wanted him to be a part of the millions of trips to the notary or the secretary of state for apostilles, a part of the many phone calls, the research, and the preparations in the house.

At times, his actions and attitudes tested and frustrated me. But in those moments, I also remembered how those traits were the same ones I admired about him. They make him successful. They allow me to stay home and are why this adoption could happen in the first place. His get-it-done attitude and gusto toward accomplishing tasks efficiently was a gift and a blessing—one for which I was sincerely grateful.

So I say again, "But God."

Every time I wanted to complain or when resentment threatened to build, Bryan turned my complaints into gratitude. He assured me all was well. With my husband's blessing, and more importantly, God's blessing, there would be one less orphan in the world.

MIRACLES DO STILL HAPPEN

As I reflected upon all God had done and how He had carefully placed each of our steps in specific order, I held tight to the one answer I knew. It was imperative that Bryan and I be on the same page about the adoption. He had agreed to the adoption, but only with recent events had he become convicted that this was right. He had acquired a deeper sense of *knowing*.

Had it not happened this way—without the conviction, the proof of God's involvement—Bryan might have questioned our life with her down the road. He might have questioned whether we had made the right decision. What if things got admittedly difficult? What if raising our daughter was harder than we imagined? Without the conviction, he might have uttered hurtful words. Doubt might have led to resentment toward me. But because of all that had happened, my rock-solid husband witnessed the hand of God in a way unlike ever before. He was convinced of his faith and his belief that God had designed this precious child as a Schumaker from the moment she was born. And even before.

God had this plan in mind long before the world began. Bryan had experienced the miraculous love God creates in the heart of an adoptive parent. He now knew he loved our little girl. He knew with

SURRENDERED HEARTS

certainty that no matter what we found on the day we would meet her face-to-face, she was ours, and we would never walk away.

My heart exploded with gratitude to God for this affirmation and for the miracle He was working in my husband's heart. This blessing would have a trickle effect for Bryan as a father to our boys, for our marriage, and especially as a father to our daughter.

The next morning, I received the call I think I'd waited for my whole life.

"There's a little girl in Bulgaria by the name of Gergana. She is the Gergana you tried to adopt six months ago. And she is the one you long to call Selah."

In fact, this precious one's file was found buried at the bottom of a stack of files on the desk of a Ministry of Justice employee. Nothing had been done with it at all. It would shortly have been moved to a file cabinet reserved for those deemed unadoptable and would have been nearly impossible for us to access again.

The date marked on that file for referral decline was the date I had logged back in to that chat group.

Only God.

Part 3

Bringing Selah Home

Are not five sparrows sold for two pennies? And not one of them is forgotten before God. Why, even the hairs of your head are all numbered. Fear not; you are of more value than many sparrows.

Luke 12:6–7 esv

Chapter 8

SEEING WHAT WE BELIEVE

I am convinced that nothing can ever separate us from God's love. Neither death nor life, neither angels nor demons, neither our fears for today nor our worries about tomorrow— not even the powers of hell can separate us from God's love. No power in the sky above or in the earth below—indeed, nothing in all creation will ever be able to separate us from the love of God that is revealed in Christ Jesus our Lord.

Romans 8:38–39 NLT

We filled out another application to the Ministry of Justice for the referral of Gergana, the child we finally knew was our Selah. We got it notarized, apostilled, and over-nighted to our agency, who forwarded it to the Bulgarian agency representing us. That agency would present it to the Bulgarian Ministry of Justice. We were told it would be another two- to four-week wait for the Ministry to meet and decide if they would approve us.

Wait. *Again.*

My flesh screamed at the prospect of waiting, yet I chose to trust. Nothing could alter God's plans. He'd proven that to me already. He would not forget us, nor would anything separate Selah or us from His love.

> Nothing could alter God's plans. He'd proven that to me already. He would not forget us, nor would anything separate Selah or us from His love.

Fighting the temptation to take back what wasn't mine, I continued the fast, finding the comfort that comes when we rest close to the beating heart of God.

Our good news was bubbling right below the surface, but we were afraid to share it yet. I remembered the pain years before of having to tell those who loved us that we had miscarried. This situation felt a lot like that. The reality was that we could still get bad news. The Ministry of Justice could still deny us a referral for Selah. We had no control over the

SEEING WHAT WE BELIEVE

situation, but we did have faith, and we had seen the miracles God had already worked on our behalf.

We wanted as many people praying for Selah and our family as possible, but the next steps remained unknown; thus, we shared our news only with those closest to us. In my wildest dreams, I could not imagine why God would give her back to us, only to take her away again. Yet the fear of repeating another story of rejection kept us quiet.

This time, as we waited, God continued to reassure us. In church, I felt the Holy Spirit move with extraordinary power. I could not stop the tears. I was overcome with emotion. I remember singing Chris Tomlin's "Our God." Each word spoke of the miracles and power of God and reminded me that He alone is able to bring light into every dark place. I felt His hand of comfort reassuring me that all would be well, that this precious girl was our Selah, our daughter. He would not allow anything to get in the way of her coming home to us now.

Later that afternoon a close friend texted me. She was excited to share with me that she had felt the Holy Spirit that very morning and was convinced that Selah would be ours. She had been praying for us during the service and felt the same presence of comfort I had felt.

The next day, exactly two and a half weeks from the day we submitted our paperwork, my telephone rang. I saw it was our caseworker. I had just picked up our boys from school, so they were in the car with me. For a brief second, I wondered if I should call her back after the boys were out of earshot. But then a holy confidence rose up. I trusted His work—what He had shown me and the reassurance from the day before.

I answered.

By this time, our sweet boys were aware of what was happening. We'd prayed together fervently for God to bring our Selah home to us. They knew disappointment was possible, but they also knew God would be there if disappointment came.

On speakerphone, our caseworker told us the good news. *We were approved.* The word the Holy Spirit had given me that first morning nine months earlier was truth. The darling girl in that picture with the infectious smile and little black ringlets framing her face was our Selah.

Laughter, tears, and shouts of joy rang out from all three of us. Our sweet caseworker couldn't help

SEEING WHAT WE BELIEVE

but join right in. These were the moments she held tightly to in her heart. When the impossible happens. When God shows up in big ways. When forever families are made.

None of us will ever forget that moment.

It reminded me to not miss the moments, to not miss when God shows up, and to not dismiss the moment as chance or coincidence. It reminded me to trace the moments back and see the pattern of a God who marks our steps and promises to make all things come together for the good of those who believe.

As I traced our moments back, I saw clear evidence of this God who loves us beyond measure. I remembered:

1. Out of the hundreds of people attempting to adopt in Bulgaria, I happened to connect with Yvonne.

2. Not only did Yvonne happen to be friends with Monica, the very woman who had received Selah's referral, but she offered to connect us.

3. I reopened my chat group account the same day Monica officially declined her referral for Selah.

4. God pointed me to the book of Ezra and the verse declaring He would hear me and show me

a straight and right way for my little ones if I humbled myself before Him and asked Him for those answers.

5. Within twenty-four hours of reading His Word and beginning the fast, I received the call from Monica giving me the detailed information I needed to clearly understand the situation.

6. Selah's case file was found at the bottom of a forgotten stack. Had it already been filed away somewhere, it would have meant more delays and the possibility of her being labeled unadoptable. She had been only days away from being lost to the world of adoption.

7. The day before the phone call from our caseworker, we received not only comfort from the Holy Spirit, but also an affirmation of that comfort through a friend.

Faith is believing in what we cannot see, but sometimes on the journey we are given the unique opportunity to witness exactly what we are believing for. *We get to witness our miracle.*

Chapter 9

GOD'S PROTECTIVE HAND

> The Lord is your keeper; the Lord is
> your shade on your right hand. The
> sun shall not strike you by day, nor
> the moon by night. The Lord will
> keep you from all evil; he will keep
> your life. The Lord will keep your
> going out and your coming in from
> this time forth and forevermore.
>
> Psalm 121:5–8 ESV

In just three weeks, we would get to meet our
now four-year-old daughter. Since Bulgaria has a
two-visit program, the first visit would be to meet
Selah and appear before a court to say we agree to
the adoption. For us, that act would merely be a for-
mality. After all God had walked us through—*nothing* we could find would make us doubt that she was
meant to be ours. The second visit would come after
all the paperwork was completed and the adoption

SURRENDERED HEARTS

had been approved. We were ready for the customary three- to five-month wait.

With gusto, we completed more paperwork. Although adoption is a hurry-up-and-wait journey, we were determined to never be the cause of delay. Stewarding this gift given to us by God was our top priority. This time, the paperwork processed so smoothly that it almost made us nervous. We completed new fingerprints (for the *third* time) for a local search and provided copies for the FBI. We updated medical evaluations and completed and mailed our request for Selah's US visa. And we completed all of this in three weeks while preparing for the week-long trip to Bulgaria. It was a whirlwind of activity.

Probably the thing I disliked most about the Bulgarian adoption program was the two-trip criterion. How could I walk away from the child I loved beyond measure? How would I walk away and leave her in an orphanage without proper love, care, and nutrition? Would it etch the wounds of abandonment deeper into her soul? Would grief consume her? Or bitterness? Would she understand that Mommy and Daddy were coming back?

I had dreaded that from the moment we signed our first papers with the program. Finally, after all

GOD'S PROTECTIVE HAND

we'd gone through in the last two years, unequivocally I had to surrender my fear and trust that this, too, was in God's capable hands. He would make all things good—somehow.

With these thoughts in mind, I sought out the best gifts I could find for our sweet girl. Ones that would help her hold on to the memories of her time with us and of the love, hugs, and kisses we would share with her for the few short days we were there.

Our daughter had never known a mother or father. At birth, her mother had left the hospital without her. Alone and unable to care for this new life, she'd

> He gave our family insight into what surrendering out of love felt like so that we, in turn, would have the ability to understand the heart of Selah's mother as she surrendered her.

done the only thing she knew to give her daughter a better chance at life.

I can only imagine the pain she felt as she walked away. It takes the desperate heart of a mother to surrender her child to an orphanage. We still pray for this woman. I pray she has come to know Jesus and has found the peace and hope only He can offer. I

SURRENDERED HEARTS

believe God knit our hearts together in the pain we shared as, in two separate instances, we surrendered our Selah. He gave our family insight into what surrendering out of love felt like so that we, in turn, would have the ability to understand the heart of Selah's mother as she surrendered her.

The boys each chose a toy for their sister—one a doll, and the other a stuffed kitten. We packed Play-Doh, stickers, miniature princess dolls, paper, coloring books, crayons, books, clothes, cookies, and candies. I found a book at our local Hallmark store that allowed me to record my voice while reading the story. It was a book with the lyrics to "Twinkle, Twinkle, Little Star."

I also created a book using pictures of her I had received from the referral, along with pictures of her brothers, dog, daddy, me, and new home. It was a simple book with a reminder of our faces and a few words of English. I purchased the board-book version so it could withstand the loving hands of curious little ones who may never have had the joy of owning a book of their own.

Along with gifts for Selah, we wanted to help meet some needs of the orphanage. I opened the request to my Facebook friends, and over the next few

GOD'S PROTECTIVE HAND

days, bag after bag of supplies arrived at our home until I didn't know how I would get it all to Bulgaria! But with careful packing, we managed to fit every bit into two large suitcases. They weighed in at 49.8 and 49.5 pounds—*just* under the fifty-pound weight limit. Whew! We packed our own clothing and necessities for the one-week trip in a carry-on. It was a superb lesson in packing light.

The agency also recommended we take gifts for those caring for Selah and those helping us through the adoption process. I searched for the perfect gifts for both the orphanage directors and caregivers. I wanted something special—something memorable that would convey our love for this beautiful child they had cared for. With that, I chose to have bracelets made for each person. Each bracelet had Selah's birthstone in the shape of a heart dangling from it. Inscribed on the back was: *With love forever, Gergana, 2010.*

Finally, everything was ready and packed, and my praying girlfriends arrived to cover our family in prayer. There is no greater gift than the gift of prayer. Just as God promises, if we call to Him, He answers. We distinctly felt His presence, and I knew deep in my heart that all would be well. We were embarking on the trip of a lifetime—one step closer to bringing our daughter home forever.

I blogged about the thoughts and emotions swirling in my head and heart during that time.

Friday, August 13, 2010—Makin' My List and Checkin' It Twice

I am finally feeling like I've checked off all the important tasks that need to be done to leave on the 28th. Whew! Now it is only the fine-tuning of all the details, like making sure I know how to Skype so we can talk with and see our boys every day. It sure is going to be difficult to leave them for almost eight days, but thanks to absolutely wonderful family and friends, I know they will be well loved while we are gone.

I don't think there will be any way around a frantic mind these last few days, though. It always seems that, no matter how well organized I try to be, the last few days before a big trip are always frantic for me . . . and this is a BIG TRIP! I

GOD'S PROTECTIVE HAND

can hardly believe that we are going to meet our little girl in merely two weeks! My heart seems to have this constant stream of emotions running through it that sometimes makes me want to burst out with a laughter-filled joy, and the next cry with that SAME joy . . . pretty crazy, I know . . . I am waaay too emotional for my sweet but logical husband. He's not sure what to make of me lately . . . but he smiles and loves me anyway. :-) So, as my heart explodes, I keep thinking . . . how her smile might look when I get to see it in real life . . . or whether there will be a sparkle in her eyes when we get to hear her giggle. I wonder if she really likes pink or if that's just what they dress her in for photos.

What might her first thoughts of us be? What will that moment be like?

And then I journey further into the future and wonder if she will like swimming in the pool as much as her brothers do and if she will want Daddy to make big waves and go with her down the slide.

I wonder what she will think of pizza and ice cream and donuts. Will she love being rocked? I wonder if she will be more of a girly girl, or will her brothers entice her into the world of action figures, dueling battles with swords, mud puddles, and fast action-packed fun?

Our sweet Selah . . . if you only knew how much we already love you . . . how you are a part of our every thought in the day . . . and how we have prayed for you for sooo long and will continue to do so for the rest of our lives, and how we dream of the day we are not a family that is separated, but a family all together right here at home.

Our Selah . . . Chosen, cherished, beloved.

"For this child I prayed." —1 Samuel 1:27 ESV

Chapter 10

GETTING TO KNOW YOU

You go before me and follow me. You
place your hand of blessing on my head.
Psalm 139:5 NLT

As we set out on our trip to Bulgaria, I promised our loved ones back home that I would continue blogging throughout the trip to journal the amazing moments we would inevitably encounter. God had given us a tribe of cheerleaders and prayer warriors who marched alongside us in the good times and in the bad. They were a gift to our family, and I wanted to make sure they were included every step of the way.

So it was in those posts on our adoption blog that I journaled our feelings of finally seeing, meeting, and holding the daughter we had already loved for what felt like a lifetime. It was there I described the incredible feeling we had of God's presence in every moment—every hug, every smile, every kiss, and every tear. And it was there—raw, emotional, and filled with ellipses and unpolished wordings—that I shared our witness to the power of prayer and the power of our mighty God.

Sunday, August 29, 2010—We Made It!

Well . . . we're here! Safe and sound . . . exhausted . . . but here, and a step closer to holding Selah!

Our morning started with a two-hour-and-forty-minute delay in Phoenix, but we made it just in time to Chicago to get on the plane for Munich. Then we arrived in Munich on time and had about thirty minutes to get to the next flight. A sweet gal who could walk faster than any other person I have ever met in my life guided us to the gate that would get us on our flight to Sofia, the largest city and capital of Bulgaria.

We boarded the plane . . . sat . . . waited. The air conditioning wasn't working and something else was wrong, so they said to deboard and in two hours it would

GETTING TO KNOW YOU

be fixed. In two hours, we reboarded and the same thing happened again. At that point, my tears started because I had been up for over twenty-four hours straight (I couldn't sleep on the flight), and we didn't know when or how we would get to Sofia. Plus, Bryan's cell phone wasn't working, and I had promised the boys we would call.

But God took care of us—gave me a nice comfy bench to sleep on for an hour, gave us a telephone through Lufthansa so we could call the boys, and then got us on a flight to Sofia. We ended up spending seven hours in the Munich airport, but we are here now, and I am going to sleep in five minutes for only about five hours until our in-country agency representative and translator pick us up in the morning and drive us to the orphanage.

AND . . . tomorrow my post will be SO MUCH BETTER because it will be about our little girl.

Selah, we're comin'!

Monday, August 30, 2010—Fallen Head over Heels

Where do I start . . . so many emotions . . . so much to say. Today was incredible. God was so present and so good. He melted our hearts even more than they were before, and all the prayers over the last few weeks asking Him to prepare her heart to know us and feel our love were answered. She responded tremendously well to us.

At first Selah was nervous, and we could see she wasn't quite sure, but within a few minutes she warmed up, and within a half hour she was giving hugs and plopping sweet kisses on our cheeks. She already knows that Daddy is the fun one and was giggling herself to death with him. It was precious. I heard her voice before I saw her, and I immediately knew it was her from the videos I have watched a million times over. That was all it took to start the tears falling . . . which was good,

GETTING TO KNOW YOU

because I had time to get it together before she came into the room. Her caretaker took her upstairs and dressed her in a cute dress to meet her "visitors." Then in walked our itty-bitty princess! She was exactly as I envisioned . . . our Selah . . . our gift from God.

We played for about an hour in the room, and then she had to leave to go eat lunch. She was hungry. She bolted for lunch, but not without giving us our hugs and kisses goodbye. She loved the baby doll and kitty from Zachary and Landon, and she absolutely LOVES Teddy Grahams and a princess candy bracelet we brought her. She fits right in as a Schumaker! She will definitely hold her own at the dessert table.

At 4:30, we were allowed to visit again, and this time we spent a couple of hours inside and then outside on the playground. She really started showing us the love at this point. She was happy and full of giggles. At the end of this visit,

SURRENDERED HEARTS

she wasn't ready to leave for dinner . . . even being hungry wasn't enough to want to walk away from us. She would only leave after we promised that we would be back in the morning . . . and then we got some more of her precious hugs and kisses and a goodbye. Then as she walked out the door, she turned and blew me a kiss. Talk about an incredible moment . . . I'm gone . . . sooo totally fallen . . . and Bryan? The tough guy who says he lives in a cave to stay the ever-solid rock . . . well, he's gone too. He is wearing his heart right on his sleeve, and his eyes show the same love I see when I watch him with our boys. This sweet child may not be ours to bring home yet . . . she may not be ours on paper yet . . . but she is ours in every other sense of the word. We love her very, very much . . . love at first sight. Thank You, Jesus!

If only Zach and Landon were here to share all this with us. We miss them so much, but we know they are doing great

GETTING TO KNOW YOU

and having a wonderful time with family and friends. Mommy and Daddy miss you guys though. We love you sooo much and can't wait to tell you more about your sister.

Later I'll have to tell you about the food here . . . yummm is all I have time for at the moment though!

Please keep praying for our little girl and that she continues to bond with us, that she somehow will understand when we leave that it is not by our choice and that we will be back just as soon as we are given permission, and that our sweet Zach and Landon continue to be filled with peace as we are gone, AND that the Nolans will find at least a moment's rest between their three kids and our two, and being my internet when I don't have it. :-)

"Trust in the LORD with all your heart."
—Proverbs 3:5 NIV

(a dear friend just reminded me of that verse . . . thank you, Leanne!)

Tuesday, August 31, 2010—Hugs, Kisses, and Lots of Giggles

Today was another amazing day . . . Sometimes I cannot believe that we are here and living this miracle. God touched my heart long ago and engraved upon it the desire to adopt a child, a daughter. He introduced me to her eight months ago and told me she was the one. My heart was broken when it didn't work out . . . but His plan was much bigger than I ever imagined, and He brought her back to us! Now here we are . . . loving her . . . holding her . . . giving and getting lots of kisses and hugs . . . and hearing a laughter that comes straight from her belly and makes our hearts bubble over every minute we are with her.

Selah is absolutely meant to be a Schumaker. Oh my stars! You should hear her laughter, and her energy definitely will give our boys some BIG competition! I had often thought I would

GETTING TO KNOW YOU

someday have a demure, quiet little girl who would just be dainty and calm . . . ohhh no! That would not be the plan. This girl has SPUNK! She loves nothing more than to race around kicking and throwing a soccer ball and thinks it is absolutely hilarious when she can manage to plunk it right on our heads . . . ESPECIALLY Daddy's.

Today they started a funny game of making faces at each other. She couldn't stop laughing. Her laughter is that kind that starts waaay down deep in her belly and completely consumes her. Precious is not even adequate to describe her laughter as I watch her and her daddy play together.

We are incredibly grateful for the presence of our translator. Even though Selah only speaks a few words in her native language of Bulgarian, she understands it completely. Our translator is an enormous help in easing Selah's fears.

SURRENDERED HEARTS

Today she also discovered how fun it is to swing up in the air while holding each of our hands. As we were walking, we did the "one, two, three . . . wheeee!" and swung her in the air. She loved it and had us do it no less than twenty times. She would even imitate our counting and say a super cute version that kind of went like *"eno, sebet, tree,* WHEEEE!"—and if we didn't respond, she had no trouble communicating that she was certainly displeased with the situation.

We were even able to call Zachary and Landon at the Nolans' before they went to school this morning. We were on the playground with Selah and wanted to be able to wish Zach our best on his karate testing and report today. It worked out wonderfully because we put them on speakerphone, and Selah heard them and said hi to them as well. She held the phone by her ear for a moment and said something that none of us could understand :-) It was neat for the boys

GETTING TO KNOW YOU

to get to hear and talk to her. She was smiling BIG. It was good for us, too, because we are missing those two little guys like you wouldn't believe.

Each day we give Selah a few more of the goodies that we brought along for her from both us and others. This morning, we gave her a cute brown-and-pink leopard-print outfit and an adorable bracelet and necklace her grandma made for her. She loved putting on the jewelry and kept saying *hubava* which means "beautiful." Her caretaker helped me with the clothing to make sure I had bought the correct size, and she was happy for Selah. She seems to love her, which gives me much comfort for when we leave.

When we came back in the afternoon, Selah was all dressed up in her new outfit and wearing her jewelry. It was so stinkin' cute! Her caretaker also told us that Selah had cried in the afternoon because she missed us and wanted us to come back. Knowing that made my heart ache for her, because I cannot stand the thought of her hurting, but it also made me rejoice in the fact that this sweet one is already bonding with us deeply. Thank You, Jesus! And thank you to all of you who have been praying for this bond to happen! Please continue to pray for that and all that is to come.

I want to again say THANK YOU to everyone who sent us off with filled suitcases for the orphanage. The director loved everything and greatly appreciated it. It made her so happy that she gave us permission to take Selah for a walk into the village where we were able to treat her to her first soda and bottled juice. She LOVED it! She did the same thing Zachary and Landon do to the straws . . . she bit them to death. She thought it was quite funny. It was such a treat to take her out of the orphanage . . . it gave us a hint of what it will be like someday when we bring her home.

GETTING TO KNOW YOU

I wish I could have taken pictures of the things everyone sent with us, but we are not allowed into the main part of the orphanage. We are only allowed on the main level with the offices and a small room where we play with Selah. I would love to get the opportunity to see the environment where she lives . . . to see the play area, eating area, sleeping area. But not even our translators are allowed there. I am told that is the rule in all the orphanages here in Bulgaria.

Please know, though, that all that love you sent with us will be felt by these children. I have seen many of them on the playground, and they are all precious beyond words. If only every child could have a family . . . seeing their eyes watch us and crave adult interaction and love breaks my heart. I pray for every child here (and all over the world) who does not have a family. I pray that God touches their hearts and shows them who He is and comforts them . . . that

SURRENDERED HEARTS

each child may know that the God of the universe, who creates all things good and beautiful, created them and loves them dearly. I pray they will know they are NOT forgotten . . . rather, they have been chosen and are cherished by their Father in heaven.

Between visits, Bryan and I went off to do some hiking and exploring. The area is beautiful. It is a mountainous region that is incredibly green with lush foliage. We climbed up a million steps and walked along a path and eventually found a beautiful park. Tomorrow we want to explore the park more because today, by the time we found it, we had to leave to go meet our translators for lunch. It seems we eat here a lot, but the food is amazing.

It consists of a lot of vegetables prepared in various ways, lots of potatoes, and meat. Cheese is on practically everything, and each of the dishes we've ordered comes with tomatoes and cucumbers alongside the entrée. I haven't seen a regular lettuce salad yet, but their salads are a mixture of various vegetables. If you aren't a vegetable person or a potato person, you would have some trouble, but we are loving it and find ourselves eating waaay too much! I thank the Lord each day for our translators, because without them, I would not have a CLUE what I was ordering. In the larger cities like Sofia, they have menus in English, but not in this village.

Until tomorrow . . . :-)

Wednesday, September 1, 2010— Reality

Reality is setting in. Today was still a miracle, and I am thankful to God for each moment He has given us . . . but the reality of our situation and the fact that tomorrow (Thursday) will be our last day with Selah before we leave keeps lurking in the back of our minds.

SURRENDERED HEARTS

Before we left this morning, I was reading in my Amplified Bible, and in it I read 2 Corinthians 3:17, which says: "Now the Lord is the Spirit, and where the Spirit of the Lord is, there is liberty (emancipation from bondage, true freedom)." God always works in such creative ways to show us the words He wants us to hear. A close friend of mine uses this verse in her own prayer life over her child, and she recently prayed that Scripture in regard to Selah and the whole adoption process. I knew when I read it that I needed to be claiming that promise from God over our Selah's life today.

When we arrived today we were alone and without our translator, so it was a different situation for Selah. When she first entered the room where we were waiting, she seemed a bit hesitant, but then she came over to us with a big hug . . . but the hug for some reason made her nervous . . . and she began to show some typical institutional behaviors. We'd seen

GETTING TO KNOW YOU

these behaviors occasionally the last few days, but today was just . . . reality. It hit me hard and to the depths of my heart . . . that this precious little girl I already love as though she had been born from me . . . has spent the last four years rocking herself or tapping her hands to the side of her head to find comfort . . . It was reality that my daughter didn't have a mommy or daddy or a special someone to pick her up when she was hurt . . . to kiss the boo-boos away, to make the scary nightmare disappear, or to simply help her through any moments of insecurity in her life. I think of all the times our boys have needed that extra time in the rocking chair or a backrub or quiet moments where they could sit on my lap and cry about the disappointments in life. She has never had that . . . instead, she has had to find a way to comfort herself. My heart grieved.

In the middle of my grieving, God reminded me to come to Him. I prayed . . . I prayed and claimed His promises for

SURRENDERED HEARTS

freedom from any hurt, ache, or emptiness from her past. I prayed for peace and joy to fill her heart. I prayed that we could meet her immediate needs at that moment. I prayed for His Holy Spirit to live in her heart . . . to reign over all her troubles . . . over all the areas where life had let her down. I held her in my arms, rubbed her back, and prayed silently.

And then God, our awesome God, met us right where we were. Peace and calm came over our little Selah, and the happy, giggly, spunky one was back with the biggest, cutest smile you could ever imagine! We'd made it through. I had the blessing of giving her physical comfort in her time of need, and God had calmed her spirit and set her free.

After that, the day went well. We read a couple of books from Grandma and played with the Play-Doh she loves so much. There's a touch-and-feel book that she was drawn to and she would rub the soft fur part of each animal listed in the

GETTING TO KNOW YOU

story to her face and say "awww!" Pure cuteness! Then we went for a walk again to the village and to the park where she had another bottle of juice, but this time she chose peach juice. She had the straw function mastered and downed that drink in less than five minutes. She was NOT setting that bottle down until it was ALL gone. From there, we went for another walk along a path to a small country church that was hundreds of years old and very pretty.

She wasn't crazy about walking uphill, so I carried her. We sang songs together and cuddled all the way up the hill. She has an incredible ability to hear a song and then hum the melody almost perfectly. She held on tight and kept holding my face and playing with my hair and giving me sweet kisses. I think my heart may burst . . . literally.

On the way down the hill, she wanted to run and have us chase her . . . I was worried because her muscle tone is

SURRENDERED HEARTS

not great, and she hasn't had many opportunities to run and develop those muscles. My worries came to fruition, and she fell and bumped her head. She had quite a goose egg on her forehead. I felt horrible! The positive was that when it happened, and I quickly picked her up and held her and tried to kiss the boo-boos . . . she calmed down. I thanked God that He has again allowed me to be her comfort.

Just as I am always thankful that He has allowed me to be the mommy to Zach and Landon and has given me the blessing of being their physical comfort, I am praising Him now that He has given me this same opportunity with Selah. She is quite an amazingly tough wee thing, though, because even with that big ol' goose egg, she finished crying and was giggling again in about five minutes.

We took her back to the orphanage because it was time for lunch. Bryan blew kisses into his own hand and then

GETTING TO KNOW YOU

pretended to gently place them in the tiny pocket of her shirt. Without us even having to explain it to her, she took the kisses out of her pocket and plopped them on her lips. Precious!

In the afternoon we went back, and Selah was immediately comfortable again. I praised God for her comfort and her peace . . . She didn't show any of the nervousness that she had that morning. It had gotten quite chilly, so we played outside a short while and then went inside to the cramped but adequate playroom. We went through every toy and every creative idea we had for the next two hours in a 5 x 10 room filled with furniture. It reminds me of waiting in a doctor's office with a small child and trying to amuse them. Bryan is sooo good at being silly, we did great. He and Selah had a blast being absolutely silly together. She cracks us up with her wild sense of humor! I think the Schumaker home is going to someday be comedy

SURRENDERED HEARTS

central, with mommy bearing the brunt of it all. :-)

As our time came to an end tonight, she went away easily because she was hungry and ready for dinner, but I guess when she realized she was going back to all the children and we weren't coming with her, she began to cry . . .

How are we going to get through the next few months?

Please, Lord, I am asking for speed in this process . . . please do not let any paperwork be delayed . . . let us all be together soon.

Chapter 11

BUT WHY, GOD?

"My thoughts are nothing like your thoughts," says the Lord. "And my ways are far beyond anything you could imagine. For just as the heavens are higher than the earth, so my ways are higher than your ways and my thoughts higher than your thoughts."

Isaiah 55:8–9 NLT

Thursday, September 2, 2010—Saying Goodbye . . . for Now

Thank you with all my heart for all the wonderful prayers. I know they helped make today much easier. Leaving was and is in no way easy . . . but we made it, and in the midst of making it, we had an absolutely precious time with Selah. God opened doors on our behalf that

SURRENDERED HEARTS

helped to bring much-needed peace to our hearts.

As soon as we arrived this morning we went inside, and our wonderful agency representative and translator asked if we could see the area where Selah lives each day. She explained to the director that it would help tremendously to bring peace to our hearts as we waited, and it would also help us to relate more to Selah's daily life. The director gave us her blessing and first invited us into her office where Selah was waiting for us. As soon as she saw us she jumped up with her big smile that fills her beautiful face. She jumped right into my arms for a hug and then into Daddy's too.

We had brought a bag of candy and enough bubble bottles for each child in the orphanage. The director let Selah hand out the treats to all the boys and girls. It was adorable . . . she loved sharing her treats and loved being in charge!

One of the caregivers then took us on a tour. We got to see Selah's sleeping area that she shares with about ten other children. All the beds were neatly made, and on her small white bed was the blanket we had brought for her. They are making sure she has it to sleep with all the time and have promised to remind her that it is from Mommy and Daddy. They showed us her personal closet and cubby, the bathrooms, and the playrooms. It was as nice as I could imagine an orphanage being in a place where they have a meager amount of money. The ladies that work there seem to care about children. They do the best they can with the little that they have.

Everything was nice and clean and tidy and organized, which helped me to understand how important routine is to her. She has lived a life following almost the same routine every single day . . . everyone is expected to do the very same thing with the group, and there

SURRENDERED HEARTS

isn't a great deal of differentiation. This is what they must do to best serve many children with few employees. So, each time we did something new or different and she would become nervous and begin rocking and tapping the sides of her face, now I knew it was because of how strange it must feel to her to be outside of this routine.

As we were touring, all the sweet little angels that live there attached themselves to us . . . they look up at you with these big sad eyes that just seem to say, *I want a family too . . . me too . . .* It is heart wrenching. I wish I could do something to ensure that each one of those angels had a family . . . There was one small boy who kept giving us hugs and literally wrapped his arms around Bryan's leg and didn't want to let go. He looked at us with the hugest brown eyes I have ever seen in my life. My big ol' solid rock of a husband had a lump in his throat . . . and I was right there with him. Maybe someone out there

BUT WHY, GOD?

reading this would love to be his forever family? I can promise you, he would melt your heart in less than one second.

We talked with the director a bit more, asking a few questions and getting such a good feeling from her. We left her our webcam, and she gave us her Skype account. We even set up times when we can Skype with Selah! How incredible is that? She also looked through the special books I made for Selah about our family and the special toys, baby doll, and a talking picture frame with all of us telling Selah how much we love her. She assured us that she would make a point of either reading the books to her herself or having one of the caretakers do it on a regular basis. She was kind to us and told us she was happy for Selah and that she could tell that we truly loved her and would take wonderful care of her. I kept smiling and crying and thanking her. When Selah was near me, I could hold in the tears, but when she wasn't, I lost that strength and the tears poured.

She understood the trouble we were having with saying goodbye, and to help ease that pain and help Selah have a bit more time with us, she let us take Selah into the village for lunch as well as our regular playtime. That gave us an extra hour! So off we went into the village to play at the park, where she headed straight to the snack stand and wanted her peach juice ... and yup ... you guessed it ... drank it down in less than two minutes! And that led to a wet diaper (they don't potty train until five), which I had to change in the middle of the park. Selah was quite uncomfortable with that. But she handled it well, and we ended up laughing together over the awkwardness of the park bench. :-)

After the park, we went to a restaurant where our translator ordered her a soup similar to what she usually eats. She ate some of it, but once she tasted

BUT WHY, GOD?

my chicken and french fries . . . the soup was history. She will definitely fit into the American way of life. She loved the little chicken bites and had to have ketchup on those french fries. She made us laugh so hard because she was doing the "raise the roof" dance move to the pop music that was playing loudly at the restaurant. She loves music a great deal and always sings along. She has such an uncanny ability to pick up the melody and rhythm. The second she heard the music, up went the hand, perfectly to the beat.

Then came the time to take her back . . . the time to say goodbye. She wanted Daddy to carry her, and he said that the closer we got, the tighter she held onto his neck. It was as if she knew something was going on. We went back to the director's office and chatted and had a last couple of giggles and lots of hugs and kisses. Bryan kept whispering in my ear to stay strong . . . I think he was doing it halfway to help me and the other half to

SURRENDERED HEARTS

help himself. We did it and made sure her last memories were of smiles. She blew us kisses and left to go take a nap. They shut the door, and again the tears fell.

I could feel God, though—I could feel His presence and His gentle reassurance that it would all be okay. I just needed to focus on the future and the still miraculous fact that this beautiful little girl was going to be ours and we were being given this incredible gift.

Friday, September 3, 2010—The Last Day

Today was our last day here in Bulgaria . . . for now. I am praying we will be back soon. I know we've got lots of awesome prayer warriors out there asking God to move the paperwork and get us back to pick up our daughter and bring her HOME.

We had to get some documents notarized this morning with our agency representative, and then the rest of the day was for us to explore. Our hearts are still stuck in that orphanage in the tiny village a couple of hours away, but we know that we need to put one foot in front of the other and make the best of each day until we get to all be together again. So, since our apartment is right downtown in Sofia, we spent the day walking MILES.

We saw all kinds of beautiful churches and old, old, OLD buildings. The history here is amazing. There are some neat things about Bulgaria, but they have much to figure out about how to get their country firmly on their feet and to find a way to help the impoverished . . . to find a way to care for and lessen the number of orphans that are here. Many times as we walked along the streets, I saw young women trying to sell goods or do other things to survive, and I thought of how one of these women could be our Selah's birth mother.

I think of the day that will come when Selah will be old enough to ask me about her mother and the inevitable "why didn't she keep me." I pray I will have the right words. I pray that whatever I say will bring peace to her soul and that none of her past will ever hinder or harm her heart, her self-confidence, her joy, or her God-given path in life.

Months ago, when I thought we had lost the opportunity to adopt her, I gave thanks to the Lord for the opportunity to pray for her throughout her life. I thought I would never meet her or know her personality, but I was ready to pray on her behalf forever. Now I have been blessed with four days with her, so not only did I meet her, but I KNOW her and love her with my whole heart.

Leaving didn't seem fair. I ached with the knowledge that our leaving could deepen the wounds of abandonment in our daughter. Laws and processes are made to protect the innocent—but too often, entirely the opposite occurs. Our little girl, who has suffered more than any child should, had to watch us walk away and wonder where we went or if we would

BUT WHY, GOD?

ever come back. Would she understand at all? Would she be angry? Would she trust us the next time?

All that had been missing was found—for her and us. Yet we had to leave it behind.

One more time to surrender. To trust. To let God hold her in His capable hands.

Chapter 12

HIS TIMING DOESN'T ALWAYS SEEM FAIR

He has made everything beautiful
in its time. He has also set eternity
in the human heart; yet no one can
fathom what God has done from
beginning to end.
Ecclesiastes 3:11 NIV

Most of us struggle with waiting. Patience is a hard-fought victory. In almost every corner of life, we are forced to hurry up, run, accomplish—quickly. The world's standards are not the same as God's, and living in the world according to God's standards is complicated. We can know we're confusing the two when we find ourselves trying to hurry God. We quickly find that God cannot be hurried. Impatience simply doesn't work in His world.

God's timing is perfect. *He* is perfect; therefore, what He *does* is *always* perfect too—including His

SURRENDERED HEARTS

timing. Even when from our side of the lens it does not look that way.

Sometimes we get to see the *why* behind the *wait*. But other times we don't. We must surrender any right to know the why and choose to unconditionally accept life as it is. We must believe that even in situations that feel desperately unfair, God is making all things right.

We were told our wait would be three to five months; then we would fly to Bulgaria and bring our baby girl home forever—home where she belongs.

> Sometimes we get to see the *why* behind the *wait*. But other times we don't. We must surrender any right to know the why and choose to unconditionally accept life as it is. We must believe that even in situations that feel desperately unfair, God is making all things right.

But our story didn't go that way. It was *seven* months before we were able to get back to Selah. A wait that, from all perspectives, appeared unfair to Selah and to us. Seven months, on top of all the months we'd missed at the front end of this process. More than a year passed between our finding her and our

HIS TIMING DOESN'T ALWAYS SEEM FAIR

bringing her home. For more than a year, she lived without us, sharing the care of one or two individuals with fifty other children. For more than 365 extra nights, she went to sleep without our stories, prayers, and kisses—and suffered more uncomforted hurts, needs, and fears.

No. It didn't look fair.

I wrestled with God, grieving the loss of more time with my daughter. I was afraid she would be mistreated and suffer from lack of care. How was it possible that these many obstacles could rise up to keep our daughter separated from us? It felt like the enemy was winning this battle, yet I knew the truth. The devil might win momentary battles, but God had already won the war.

Arriving back home, we expected to quickly connect by phone or Skype as the director had promised. It took over two months before our first call went through. Finally, one morning in early November, a Bulgarian voice answered our Skype call. On the other side was the director we had met with and our Selah sitting right on her lap! There were the little black ringlets of hair, along with the rosy cheeks and firecracker eyes.

SURRENDERED HEARTS

My heart skipped a beat. It was real. There she was.

For the next seven weeks, we were gifted these moments. Moments of giggles, smiles, and many declarations of *I love you*. We prayed God was reassuring Selah that we would come back. And we prayed His presence would be the arms to hold her when ours were unable.

But just as surprisingly as the calls were answered, they abruptly stopped. Our last Skype call was on Christmas. With no forewarning, they stopped answering our calls. Then a few long weeks later, a telephone call went through. The voice at the other end found Selah and brought her to the phone. But there were no giggles. No joy. She cried and wouldn't stop. Then, with the limited Bulgarian I had learned, I heard the voice tell Selah to shut up, and the phone went dead. From that day forward, we didn't hear another word from the orphanage until the day in April we went to pick her up.

The enemy taunted me with fear. He wanted me to doubt, to believe our God wasn't good and wouldn't make this right. He wanted the grief to consume my faith.

His Timing Doesn't Always Seem Fair

It seemed every obstacle possible was set before us. Things unheard of in this process continued to happen. Papers mysteriously disappeared or went unapproved for no known reason, sometimes in the States and sometimes in Bulgaria. I contacted government representatives in the United States to help us. Then, when the struggles landed on the Bulgarian side, I contacted the US embassy there for help. At each step, just as weariness began settling, we'd find the breakthrough. It was as though the enemy pushed, and God allowed it until He knew I had no more to give—and then He'd send in an angel in disguise. Usually it was a random government official who pulled strings and made the impossible happen.

At one point, a judge in the Bulgarian court decided that the six sets of fingerprints and FBI clearance reports were insufficient, and therefore, she would not approve our adoption. This judge knew that the highest level of clearance for Americans comes from the FBI. She had approved many other adoptions. Bryan and I had nothing more than a speeding ticket attached to our names. There was no logical reason to doubt our credentials. But she said no. And the worst part was that we were expected to present more documentation when court reconvened the following

SURRENDERED HEARTS

week—yet she didn't tell us what would suffice. The attorneys in Bulgaria and our agency representatives here in the States were baffled. If we didn't meet the judge's requirements, though, we wouldn't be granted the adoption of Selah.

That's when I made a phone call to the US embassy in Bulgaria. After telling my story several times, my call was forwarded to a man named Michael. God had placed him in that spot on that day for a reason. He would be the hands and feet of Jesus for us. Michael found our paperwork and verified our high-level clearance, as well as the accuracy and sufficiency of all our work. He was perplexed and concerned about the situation. So he decided to do more than make a telephone call.

Michael paid the judge a personal visit.

Tuesday, February 15, 2011 — One More Week of Waiting in Faith

(Written by Coleen Nolan)

Today's call was not exactly what Lori and Bryan were hoping for … but they are fixing their eyes of faith on the light at the end of this tunnel. The judge in Bulgaria has committed to approve Selah's adoption on Monday. Yes, six more days of waiting in hope and trusting in God's faithfulness until she is officially Selah Schumaker.

One highlight of the call was that the Monday after that (2/28), her birth certificate will be issued, which is an exciting change from what they had been told before. Birth certificate wait time used to be two to three weeks. Travel should be scheduled one to two weeks from February 28.

As a friend who has traveled the adoption journey, I simply cannot imagine the ache that Lori and Bryan and their boys have carried . . . wanting their little girl home so desperately, yet living the challenge of a system that at times seems set against this princess's new life in her forever family. Surely, many of you have struggled like the Schumakers when God's timing does not seem to make sense at all. We believe with all we are the truth found in

SURRENDERED HEARTS

His Word that says His ways are higher—yet everything inside us sometimes cries out for things to move along.

I thought about Job 23:10 today. Check it out. After countless struggles and so much frustration, Job says, "He knows the way I take; when he has tested me, I will come forth as gold." Bryan and Lori have had an adoption journey like no other. They have been tested and tried and tested again. And each of us who loves them has been challenged by their unyielding faith and humbled by their relentless pursuit of a little girl who sits today in an orphanage in Bulgaria. I look at them, and I see gold. Pure gold. They are living testimonies of God's love . . . love that never gives up, never loses faith, is always hopeful, and endures through every circumstance.

So today we stand again with the Schumakers. We pray and cry out for the next six days. We believe with them that in six days a little girl's name will be changed. And not just her name, but her

His Timing Doesn't Always Seem Fair

destiny. We long for the moment when we can rejoice together that our girl is coming home to be loved and treasured by so many of us.

And we will give our God—the One who makes all things right and whose timing is perfect—all the glory.

Coleen

Tuesday, February 22, 2011—Trying to Believe

Our judge did not follow through with her commitment on Monday. We found out late Monday that she hadn't gone into work that day, so we had to wait till today to see what she would do. The call came today saying that she changed her mind again and is requesting an official letter from the US embassy verifying that the FBI clearance is the highest level of security in the United States. Her meeting with the representative from the embassy was not sufficient.

SURRENDERED HEARTS

We are crushed, stunned, disappointed, frustrated . . . completely brokenhearted. I wrote a letter today imploring the embassy to help us in this matter. Our hands feel tied . . .

I have sat and tried to find insight into the judge's perspective . . . does she know that this child has spent way too many days, weeks, months, years in an orphanage without a family? Does she have any idea of how great our love is for this child? Does she have any idea that we would do anything within our own physical power to bring her home? Does she realize our hearts have a huge hole in them, filled with the grief of not having her home yet? If only I could get her to understand this . . . then maybe she would not do this to us or to any other family ever again.

I know I have to believe that the time will come. Selah will be ours. I need to stay strong and keep my faith. I know my faith is there, but it feels like it is in a million

HIS TIMING DOESN'T ALWAYS SEEM FAIR

pieces around me. I keep getting back up and putting it back together, but then the next wave of emotion comes and knocks it all down again. But I'm going to keep picking up the pieces, and I am going to keep trusting the Lord and believing He will bring Selah home. I am going to praise Him for all the blessings in my life. I will praise Him for showing me the true heart of adoption . . . showing me a love that I never understood before . . . giving me a glimpse of the love He has when He adopts us into His family. It is a powerful love. It can move mountains, and that is the promise I am going to hold onto . . . and never let go.

With my hope threatened, I reached out to the embassy again. And once again, Michael stepped up. I don't know what he said or what happened, but this time the judge agreed.

Friday, February 25, 2011 — It's Really True. Selah Is Coming Home!

Okay . . . I'm having to stop the tears of joy to write this right now! We just received the most wonderful news that we are officially the parents of a beautiful Bulgarian princess! I introduce you to Selah Gergana Schumaker!

I cannot believe how absolutely blessed we are to be given this precious daughter. I know there have been moments where my faith was shaken, my patience unwound, and my heart broken . . . but God—aren't those awesome words?— But God moved the mountains. He has parted our Red Sea, and we will be rushing across that open road He carved for us just as soon as we can!

We have to wait for the completion of Selah's certificate of adoption and then we can travel. I pray the wait is not long, but now I can surely see the moment coming when I can wrap her in my arms

Monday, March 14, 2011 — Gotcha Day Is April 4, 2011!

and never have to walk away again. The moment we can truly be a family!

We have our official travel dates. We leave April 2 and return April 9. It feels almost surreal. I'm almost afraid to fully feel the joy . . . the guards around my heart are not wanting to let go. But let go they must . . . because Selah is comin' home!

Last week had some bleak moments when we learned there had been an error on our court decree and that would cause another delay. *Delay* was not a word my heart could handle very well. There were more tears and then plain ol' anger . . . but in the end, the delay was only two extra weeks from our initial tentative dates. As it turns out, Gotcha Day will be exactly seven months from the time we left our sweet girl.

SURRENDERED HEARTS

Seven months is a long time. It is forever in the life of a four-year-old. My brain and heart have run wild lately. I started letting my mind think things that are absolutely contrary to the Word of God. I worried about the loss of developmental time, the loss of bonding time, the loss of intervention time, the loss, the loss, the loss.

But God ever so gently filled my heart with the reminder that He is God, the very same One who created the universe. Time is not of concern to Him. He is bigger than time. He is bigger than any loss I can ever come up with. He has a plan for Selah, and there is nothing in this world that can stop that plan . . . not four and a half years, not misplaced paperwork, not difficult judges, and certainly not another timing delay!

A few months before we began our adoption process, the group Salvador released a song called "Aware." I fell in love with it because it calls out to God,

HIS TIMING DOESN'T ALWAYS SEEM FAIR

asking Him to make us aware of how He is in every detail of our lives—from the small to the big, from the insignificant to the life-changing.

I prayed God would break my heart for what breaks His and that He would make me so aware of His presence in my life that I would never forget that it is He in me who makes all things possible.

He has answered that prayer tenfold. I have learned over and over again that He is in every detail. He has been there in times of joy and in times of sadness. He has loved me when I was angry at others and even angry at Him. He has forgiven me for each sinful thought, word, and deed throughout the last two years and especially throughout the last few months! And now, as we prepare for the last leg of this journey with Selah, I am eternally thankful.

Chapter 13

SELAH: CHOSEN, CHERISHED, BELOVED

You alone created my inner being. You knitted me together inside my mother. I will give thanks to you because I have been so amazingly and miraculously made. Your works are miraculous, and my soul is fully aware of this. My bones were not hidden from you when I was being made in secret, when I was being skillfully woven in an underground workshop. Your eyes saw me when I was still an unborn child. Every day of my life was recorded in your book before one of them had taken place.

Psalm 139:13–16 GW

The enemy uses many things in this world to convince us that we are unworthy and, even worse, unlovable. Broken people and broken families are some of his favorite tools. From one generation to the next, somewhere along the road, children are hurt. Children are left alone and without the love they need to fully develop and thrive.

The world of adoption has opened my eyes to some ugly and painful aspects of life. But it has also enabled me to see the power of God, the power of His love, and the power of embracing who we are as His children and seeing ourselves in His reflection.

Who Is Going with Us?

We left Landon with Grandma and Grandpa, and with just-turned-nine Zach in tow, we left for Bulgaria early on the morning of April 2. We hadn't originally planned to take Zach with us because of the long hours of travel and the significant extra cost—not to mention the unknowns we were sure to discover once we arrived. But he, with his profound gift of argumentation, convinced us otherwise.

SELAH: CHOSEN, CHERISHED, BELOVED

Months before, at only eight years old, he'd presented his case. He explained how he needed to be there to see Selah's country and her orphanage. Wanting to be the best big brother possible, he argued the necessity of personally seeing her past and being there those first moments that she was ours. He told us she would need him when she was scared. And he told us if we took the time to pray and read God's Word, we would know he needed to go with us. God told him so.

He was right. How could we argue that from an eight-year-old?

The flights all went smoothly, and after about thirty hours of door-to-door travel, we arrived at our apartment in Bulgaria. In six hours, our representative would pick us up, and we'd begin the three-hour drive into the mountains to pick up our daughter. We were one step closer to the moment forever would begin. The moment we would wrap our arms around her and promise to love her forever. The moment we would begin reminding her every day that she is our Selah—*chosen, cherished, and beloved.*

I don't think I slept at all that night. Bryan and Zach seemed to do a better job of it, but I was not able to turn off the thoughts circulating through my mind.

The Final Step

Our driver arrived just as promised. With our gift-filled luggage in hand, we piled into his car. The three-hour drive turned into four as we picked up another parent heading to a different orphanage for his first visit. Bryan and I kept stealing glances at each other. We were nervous.

After all the challenges we had faced, we were well aware that obstacles are plentiful and the possibility of another one was plausible. What if we arrived at the orphanage and Selah wasn't there? We were well aware at this point that anything was possible. On the other hand, we also knew God had delivered us thus far. And here sat Selah's big brother with the biggest grin on his face because he couldn't wait to meet his sister.

Around one mountain and then another, we traveled the winding road. Then we saw it—Нареченски Бани—the sign for the tiny but picturesque village that housed our daughter's orphanage. We passed the hotel where we'd stayed on our previous trip to Narechenski Bani, and then, another short distance past, we turned onto the road leading to her.

SELAH: CHOSEN, CHERISHED, BELOVED

My heart was pounding. I kept whispering, "Selah, we're coming." Zach held my hand. And together, Bryan, Zach, and I prayed for our reunion.

My memories of the orphanage were mostly fond. However, concern had set in. I had discovered that the director we met when we first visited was an assistant. The primary director had been absent during our visit, and what I'd learned of her in the meantime wasn't encouraging. It explained the difficulty in communication and the disturbing cries that had ended our last conversation with Selah. They had left my spirit in a state of unrest.

We parked and walked up to the gated entrance, waiting for permission to enter. Guided to a small hallway, we waited. Eventually we were led to the director's office. There were no familiar or comforting faces from our last visit. This director was all business, without a smile or warmth. We presented the suitcases full of the requested toiletries, over-the-counter medications, and school supplies for the children. She went through the suitcases, sorting and organizing our contributions. Then she called for workers to carry it away.

SURRENDERED HEARTS

At this point, we still hadn't seen our daughter. Everything within me cried out to hold her. The wait of these remaining moments was almost unbearable.

We were allowed some questions and given some answers. And sadly, the conversation we shared in those moments both broke me and angered me. My unsettled spirit had not merely been the symptom of a worried mom. It was God conveying to me that our daughter desperately needed us now more than ever. Holding back tears, we signed a plethora of paperwork. Then, *finally*, the moment we had long dreamed about became a reality.

A lifetime of knowing.

Decades of praying.

Years of paperwork, research, and planning.

Lots of tears.

And the growing of faith, while we waited.

Forever had come.

On April 4, 2011, Selah Gergana Schumaker came around the corner in the arms of a caregiver. I reached out to her, and she reached back to me. Holding her tightly, I promised I would never leave her again. She was forever a Schumaker and loved beyond measure.

SELAH: CHOSEN, CHERISHED, BELOVED

She would never again know life without a family. That day began her journey to learning who she is, *whose* she is, and that she is chosen, cherished, and beloved.

It was as if a part of her understood. She held tight to us and didn't look back. There were no goodbyes. It didn't appear our girl had attachments to anyone at all. Then, at the last moment, a familiar face. The assistant director who had tried her best to love Selah well walked into the room. She looked at me with tears in her eyes. Something unspoken passed between us as we left the facility.

Selah climbed into the car with us to begin her new life. No looking back. Only looking forward.

When God is the author of our story, nothing can separate us from Him. Not any kind of red tape or evil that walks this world. Not incompetence, miscommunication, or financial obstacles. Not language or time. Nothing. *Nothing is bigger than our God.*

As we drove away, I understood my heart far better than before. I realized the picture wasn't fully complete. God had already walked us a tremendous distance, and now He hinted that what remained extended beyond the here and now. But in those moments as our Selah joined us, I understood the story He was writing.

SURRENDERED HEARTS

A story of learning about surrender and learning to trust. The kind of faith that says I trust

- in God's timing.
- when everything around me screams of injustice.
- although chaos swirls about me.
- as my body, mind, and soul want to respond in fear.
- that somehow or someway it will all be okay.

For me and for many others, this trust means repeatedly surrendering our version of how the story should go. I wasn't the author or designer of our story. I learned as I walked toward our daughter

> I learned as I walked toward our daughter that God would only give me enough light to see the next step. And that had to be enough.

that God would only give me enough light to see the next step. And that had to be enough. Surrendering allowed me to walk a journey of faith that led me to the beautiful daughter God had marked as ours long before the beginning of time. And I wonder, *If we all lived a surrendered life, what beauty might we be led to?* And to juxtapose that thought, *If we don't surrender, what might we miss out on?*

Closing Words

Tragically, in the hours after getting Selah to our apartment in Sofia, we found she was not as we had left her seven months earlier. She was malnourished and exhibited signs of abuse. Amid moments of joy and laughter, fear threatened to consume her. Because we were in a foreign country and fearful of anything stopping us from taking her home, we couldn't relay the truth of what was happening. I had to find the joyful moments and write of those at the time to everyone at home praying and cheering us on. Only a small group of trusted prayer warriors and confidants knew the full truth of the situation.

We also discovered significant medical conditions that had been neither treated nor reported. We arrived in the United States on Saturday evening, April 9, 2011. Monday morning, I was waiting outside our pediatrician's doors when they opened. Our world turned upside down again, and we were called

SURRENDERED HEARTS

once again to deepen our faith and continue to surrender. We searched for a new normal amid a world of hospitals, doctors, specialists, therapists, medications, and treatments.

Becoming an adoptive family to a child with significant medical, mental, and developmental special needs wasn't what we had foreseen. Nor was it an easy transition. Maybe God will have me share that story someday in the future; I don't know. But we have no regrets. God has worked, is working, and will continue to work miracles in our daughter. There is no limit to what He can do. Our Selah has come remarkably far, and we know beyond the shadow of a doubt that she will continue to move forward.

I look back and remember when I first heard the word *selah* used as a name. I knew then that if we ever adopted a girl, that would be her name. I even told Bryan that, and he just smiled and kind of did a half eye-roll, when he wasn't yet convinced about adoption. But as I looked into the word, I found that it is used in Scripture to indicate a moment of pause, a time to reflect upon God's goodness and give Him praise. Could there be a better name?

When the wait seems impossible, when the obstacles are large, when discouragement threatens, or

CLOSING WORDS

when the challenges seem too intense, her name reminds us to stop and praise.

Selah is our reminder to celebrate and praise the One who is always good.

Today, she knows Jesus, and she knows He loves her. Selah knows she has a family who will move heaven and earth for her and that, no matter what, they will never stop loving her.

That's what a surrendered heart is all about.

My Heart for You

I pray this book has blessed you and gives you courage to live with a surrendered heart in your circumstances. No matter what your story, when you live a surrendered life to Christ, He will lead you to the most precious of treasures.

For more encouragement and bonus book features, you can find me at www.LoriSchumaker.com/Surrendered-Hearts-Book. Available materials include:

1. Prayers for the adopting family.
2. Bible verses to hold in your heart during your adoption.
3. " . . . but the Greatest of These is Love —1 Corinthians 13:13" original print.

SURRENDERED HEARTS

4. Scripture cards of all the Bible verses used in this book.
5. Resource lists, including
   a. books to help you prepare for the adoption journey,
   b. children's adoption books, and
   c. adoption websites.

Photos

The first picture I saw of our little girl.

Outside view of the orphanage.

Outside view of orphanage grounds.

Orphanage

Selah and her daddy. There was an immediate bond.

Reading in the small 6x4 room during our third day.

Our daughter.

Driving up the street to the orphanage. Almost there now.

Finally in my arms forever.

Zachary and Selah's first moment.

She knew he would love her forever.

A very weak and weary little girl. Arriving home at last.

Landon waiting for his family to come home.

Landon and Selah's first moment.

One month later, and she already knew these boys would move heaven and earth for her.

Our family is complete.

A glowing Selah, after being home for only eighteen months.

Surrendered HEARTS

- Prayers for the Adopting Family

- Bible Verses for Your Adoption Journey

- "... but the greatest of these is love -1 Cor 13:13" original print.

- Scripture Cards of all Scripture in Surrendered Hearts

- Resource Lists

Bonus Resources for the Adoptive Parent found at www.LoriSchumaker.com/Surrendered-Hearts-Book

Order Information

To order additional copies of this book, please visit
www.redemption-press.com.
Also available on Amazon.com and BarnesandNoble.com
or by calling toll-free 1-844-2REDEEM.